Business Development for the Biotechnology and Pharmaceutical Industry

For Clare

Business Development for the Biotechnology and Pharmaceutical Industry

MARTIN AUSTIN

GOWER

Published by
Gower Publishing Limited
Wey Court East
Union Road
Farnham
Surrey GU9 7PT
England

Ashgate Publishing Company
Suite 420
101 Cherry Street
Burlington, VT 05401-4405
USA

British Library Cataloguing in Publication Data
Austin, Martin
  Business development for the biotechnology and
  pharmaceutical industry
  1. Biotechnology industries 2. Pharmaceutical industry
  I. Title
  615.1'0684

  ISBN 978-0-5660-8781-3 (Pbk)

Library of Congress Cataloging-in-Publication Data
Austin, Martin.
  Business development for the biotechnology and pharmaceutical industry / by Martin Austin.
    p. cm.
  Includes bibliographical references and index.
  ISBN 978-0-566-08781-3
  1. Biotechnology industries. 2. Pharmaceutical industry. I. Title.

  HD9999.B442A97 2008
  615.1068'4--dc22

                                                                            2007051369

Mixed Sources
Product group from well-managed forests and other controlled sources
www.fsc.org Cert no. SGS-COC-2482
© 1996 Forest Stewardship Council

FSC

Printed and bound in Great Britain by
TJ International Ltd, Padstow, Cornwall.

Contents

List of Figures

Foreword

This book has come about through the creation of a course in pharmaceutical business development. In 2004 I met with Luc de Lange who was establishing CELforPharma – a new management training firm where he is the CEO. Luc was seeking new courses for the new company. He had identified that no specific courses were being offered for the industry in the area of business development and asked if I could develop such a course for him. The result is a 2-day course which covers largely the same content as this book and has evolved since the initial versions to be a high-level overview of business development with special emphasis on the needs of the pharmaceutical and biotechnology industry. In developing that course I received a great deal of help from Luc in refining the structure and delivery of the messages. Over the last 3 years we have focused on the issues that the delegates have identified as the most interesting and relevant to them, and these are reflected in this book. Therefore, rather than attempt to explain every nuance of the techniques and tools required to develop businesses in the industry, I have tried to provide the same kind of 'illustrated tour' of the structure of a licensing transaction with an occasional detour into mergers and acquisitions or financing. The course now also runs twice a year in China in association with David Xue of Pharmaguys Ltd, Beijing. I have since developed an expanded 4-day version of the course which is presented with a faculty of colleagues from the industry as the 'European Course on BioBusiness Development' (ECBD) and is run under the auspices of the University of Basel as an elective module in the Masters in Advanced Studies in Drug Development Sciences offered by the university under Professor Fritz Bühler.

Business development in the pharmaceutical industry is a topic which is too broad and diffuse to try and encapsulate comprehensively in a single volume and I cannot hope to provide a description for more than a fraction of the possible variations in deal structure and techniques used. So, drawing on the continuing popularity of the pharma business development course, I offer some of the experiences I have had and stories I have heard which can act as a broad checklist for those trying to bring their own deals to a successful close. I'm sure I will have missed many items and issues but I hope the book will act as a reasonable guide to help colleagues plan their business development deals and other transactions and avoid some of the worst pitfalls while en route.

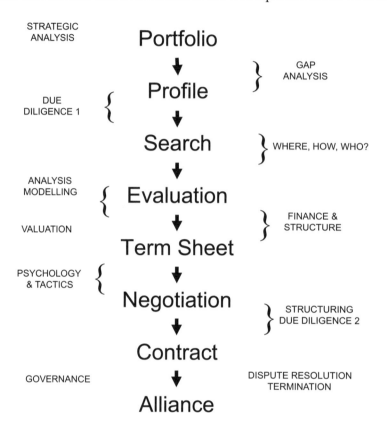

Figure 0.1   The structure of the book

The Role of Business Development

Defining business development

What is 'business development'? This is usually the first question I have to answer whenever I'm asked what I do for a living by people outside the pharmaceutical industry. The answers I try to give are often tailored to the audience and what they are likely to quickly understand from their own experience. However, as few people have any idea that such a role exists beyond some hazy idea of marketing they usually smile politely and suddenly remember there is someone on the other side of the room to whom they must say hello immediately. So a definition of business development, at least as I have seen it performed since it comes in many different guises, will be useful. I define it as 'any activity that alters the status quo of the business'. This includes activities such as:

- planning

- adding for growth

- subtracting for profit

- business process improvement

- competitive awareness and advantage.

Planning is a central activity to business development because, as a friend once told me, 'There is no worse combination than great tactics and a lousy strategy – you just make things worse faster.' In order to plan well, the business developer will need to have or obtain a number of skills and resources and these will be the subject of later chapters. However, a base set of skills for the business developer include being well organized, having a good breadth of knowledge, imagination, being good at analysis in different forms and having good communications skills, particularly listening and interpretation. Good organization means not just being able to collect information but to collate it, recall it and relate it. I have had the advantage of having worked briefly in IT with database designers and seen how the discipline of having a process for each of these activities creates a systematic approach. These processes can be made into a computer program. Addressing the information needs of planning in a systematic way brings organization to the planner and helps in structuring their communications to their own organization and to their counterparties in any negotiations.

Imagination is required because, while the pharmaceutical industry is at the pinnacle of scientific and technical innovation, bringing this science to market needs creativity and application. Business developers must look beyond the technology and into the future. This requires forecasting: seeing the combination of products or of processes or even of companies to create more value, which is needed to develop the business.

Solid planning enables one to say 'What if?' about tomorrow. For instance, if our sales are €100 million today, what might happen next year if: a competitor doubles their promotion or brings a new product to market; perhaps a new surgical technique enters the market; two competitors merge and become more powerful or any number of other potential events? Many businesses have failed, or failed to thrive because they did not plan well, which means looking high and low and far and wide at their situation. It is business development that has this responsibility in both large and small companies. Companies that become bound up in their own technology and so see only their nearest competitors and local markets can limit not just their vision but their potential as well.

Planning offers different choices; choices to add new products or companies to their portfolio for growth, or, if the company is mature, to sometimes 'subtract for profit' by dividing products and spinning off activities which are diverting resources or diluting profit or growth. You may ask, 'Why do large companies sell off product lines which are profitable?' The reason is that just as gardeners cut off healthy branches which are growing in the wrong direction or making more wood and leaves than fruit, the company must be 'trimmed' to produce a better result; particularly if the company is publicly traded. This may involve divesting itself of a slow-growing older brand to concentrate on new fast-growing products. The result will allow the chairman to point to rapid growth and a reduced reliance on products under threat of generic or other competition; shedding lower profit divisions or business units will also focus a company's activities on what is the heart of its business.

Close analysis of the company's plans can also reveal deficiencies in business processes. When seeking reasons as to why next year's growth cannot be more than 'x' per cent, or why last year's growth was only 'y' per cent, it may be that there is insufficient manufacturing capacity or that the supply chain cannot perform fast enough. It may also be that orders can't be processed or shipped fast enough or that orders are not being generated at sufficient speed. In each of these cases the business development function should be taking the lead in identifying the problem and proposing solutions.

With the skills to collate and organize the data required for analysis and the imagination to see why the company is where it is, and what could be done to improve and increase the top and bottom lines, the business developer has an important role in the strategy and direction of the company. There is a further major role for business development: as the company's champion, someone who monitors competition. Business developers need to be very aware of threat and competition, sources of which include:

- internal constraints
    - inertia
    - distraction

- age and time

- direct competitors

- indirect competitors

- external constraints
    - external inertia
    - distraction

- new competitors

- task focusing.

Competition comes in many forms. Perhaps the most galling is the negative effect of internal competition; the inertia in an organization which is best expressed by the old saying, 'familiarity breeds contempt'. When parts of the organization settle for 'the way we've always done it', and 'the easiest way', then the company is not trying to improve its product. Many parts of an organization can become guilty of this and manufacturing and administration, two of the non-'frontline' groups, are particularly prone to it. Administrative functions tend to encourage inertia: the tedium of the task of shifting invoices and processing orders divorces staff from the reality of the market and the older a product is the less attention it gets in the organization. Years ago, as a product manager for older products (a good training ground for business development), I frequently had to go and unblock the system where stacks of orders or dockets or whatever had been sidelined because of some other priority or just through volume of work and 'not enough resources'. This cry of not enough resources is a favourite among researchers and in manufacturing too. Manufacturing functions are often diverted by minutiae since in any function there is a bewildering array of distracting events which are constantly present. Completion of each part of the project may be delayed because one thing or another has to be fixed first. Of course, all of these problems would be solved if only they had 'more resources'.

I list these distractions and sublimations as competition because like friction they slow down the business and so require the attention of the business developer every bit as much as does the competition that emanates from the outside world.

Idleness and distraction are also powerful competitive forces in their own right because the variation in peoples' underlying natures, before they are grouped together as customers, divides them into categories affecting the business development landscape (see Figure 1.1).

In planning, the unseen market competitors are rarely featured as drivers in a market yet as barriers to entry they form sometimes insurmountable hurdles. Distraction, which is given negligible attention when compared to direct competition, occurs in the external market because people are overwhelmed with information.

A company's business developer needs to be aware of direct and indirect competition as actors and factors in terms of the market as well as in specific product challenges. It may be that the market opportunity can be treated by different modalities such as in the treatment of metabolic diseases like type II diabetes. Modifying someone's diet so that they lose weight can be

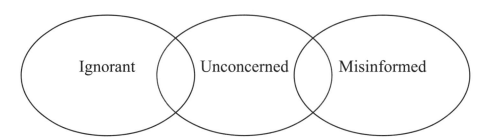

Figure 1.1   Unseen market competitors

an effective way of controlling their diabetic symptoms and, while weight-reducing foods may not seem to be a major component of the market, new functional foods are being developed which are likely to increase in the use of one modality over another, not involving a pharmaceutical product and could reduce the number of patients who should be considered as treatable in a market forecast. Similarly, cellular therapies that introduce new islet cells to the pancreas through various means are in the clinic and could also soon impact the direction of the market.

In oncology the introduction and development of new products is quite intense. The number of patients available for treatment will be linked only to those entering therapy once those who have existing disease are treated. Many market models seen at investor conferences fail to take into account the fact that the available market for new biological therapies may be reduced because of advances in other areas such as radiotherapy or surgery.

Even activities of the industry which are not intended as competition can have competitive effects. When a product for thrombolytic therapy was being evaluated it became apparent that the market was being severely depleted by the number of clinical trials being held for different agents, including the US National Institute of Health (NIH), which was attempting to establish the value of the therapeutic approach itself. Since there are only 1.5 million acute myocardial infarctions (heart attacks) per annum in the USA then, after discounting those whose heart attack occurred too far away from major treatment centres to be useful, the number of new patients who would benefit from such therapy was some 250,000 per annum. Seven trials, each of which recruited 10–15,000 patients, were therefore leaving few patients to be treated on a paying basis.

Business developers must therefore learn and apply their skills appropriately.

While they need to be aware of the situation of the company on the basis of historical data, they must also be capable of projecting future scenarios for the company in a multifaceted and multivariate environment with independently moving elements and competitors who will react to any change made by the company. Plans made to change the company must be flexible.

The skills base for business development has three distinct areas: knowledge, analysis and communication.

Knowledge

Industry-specific knowledge is required in six key areas:

- research

- manufacturing

- the supply chain

- development

- sales and marketing

- finance.

RESEARCH

Knowledge of the research process does not mean that the business development person must be either a scientist or have performed this role. Some understanding of the biological basics of a drug's action – and so the comparative strengths and weaknesses this could bring to a marketed product – is crucial however for evaluating or valuing a product for sale or for licensing.

MANUFACTURING

Manufacturing constraints and processes are a major component of a product's value. Inherent complexity in a manufacturing process can become a protection if the know-how specific to a process is kept confidential or if it is patented. Such complexities might, however, be constraints and so a barrier to licensing the product. When considering a product, awareness of its ease of manufacturing is a vital component for the business developer.

THE SUPPLY CHAIN

The supply chain, especially logistics management, is another component which affects product value and again is often overlooked. Yet physical barriers have real effects on business. I was once left with no alternative but to fly 10 tonnes of an active ingredient from the US across the Atlantic to the Denmark because of inflexibility in supply chain. My product, a bulk-forming laxative, was selling well and exceeding forecasts, but the bulk-forming agent was being sourced from India by ship, then landed at New Orleans, taken by barge up to be milled in Chicago and shipped back down the Mississippi and then off again by ship to Denmark for irradiation before being transferred to the UK for packaging near Newcastle. To speed up the process when Newcastle began to run out of product for packaging we were forced either to airfreight to Denmark or to lose market share in the middle of the launch – we had no real choice.

DEVELOPMENT

Development also has many different aspects, each with its own nomenclature for the practices and regulations involved. Indeed these regulations are a broad subject in themselves as they must define each step from pre-clinical work in lead identification then optimization, formulation and initial batch creation. Development moves on to follow a list of stages and clinical events such as initial trial design and toxicology, carcinogenicity studies, proof of concept in animals, entry into man, clinical trial design, statistics for the powering of studies, regulatory approval of trial design and processes approval for market. However, the overarching concern is the clinical trial design for it is this which will determine if the product can demonstrate the safety, efficacy and competitive advantage that will permit it to be marketed for the desired disease area, and under what conditions. Only if the design will produce the appropriate evidence can the value of the product to be fully exploited.

SALES AND MARKETING

Business development has a pivotal role in understanding the language and limitations of development methods and translating the needs of the market into a design which can produce data to satisfy the regulators. If the trial end-points are too narrowly defined and produce results which are statistically inconclusive, a valuable product can be withheld from the market while extra trials are performed, or lost entirely if the costs are too high. Part of the knowledge required to create the product labelling therefore must come from a deep knowledge of the market as a sales medium. The process of marketing and selling medicines involves a structured series of events orchestrated in such a way as to introduce each of the players in the market to the new product, demonstrate its place in therapy, encourage first use and then, based on that experience, incorporate the product as a daily therapeutic choice. The market is made up of customers with needs and how to address those needs is the end-point of the design of the clinical trials. Putting the right evidence in the hands of the salesperson is one of the most critical parts of developing a business. If the product and its message are not well understood and well designed then all other efforts will have been wasted. Products do not sell themselves.

FINANCE

The business developer must understand the financing and financial consequences of all of the elements in the chain, which may start with the conception of a company as the means to commercialize academic research through to its establishment, product developments and commercialization in a market all the way to the distributions of profit and dividends to shareholders. Working with accountants, bankers, financiers, auditors and the rest requires the business developer to have insight and understanding of their methods. The business developer must understand the implications of one choice over another in the execution of licensing deals, the acquisition of companies, capital expenditure and taxation.

All of this may seem a huge amount of knowledge to acquire. Part of the purpose of this book is to provide a route map to some of the as yet unexplored regions you will possibly visit in your next deal.

Analytical skills

The second area of skills required are analytical skills, I have broken these down into four basic areas:

- process

- pattern

- numerical skills

- heuristic skills.

PROCESS ANALYSIS SKILLS

Process analysis looks at the logical sequence in a model where for instance the forecast for a product can be derived from a set of reasonably 'hard' data (such as epidemiological data sets, perhaps of disease incidence, prevalence or death rates). Knowing the numbers of patients suffering from a particular disease such as stress urinary incontinence (SUI), one can state various assumptions which are either fact-based or logical and from this produce a forecast (see Figure 1.2).

Another way of approaching this is to read a counterparty's licensing term sheet as if you had written it, looking not just for what it says but for what is omitted, either deliberately or by mistake, and so work out your counter-proposals to match their desires with your own. The term sheet is just a sketch of the final agreement and so there is much room for manoeuvre as the negotiation is planned.

Targeted patients (in millions) in the three key markets

		2008	2009	2010	2011	2012	2013	2014	2015
Population (m) (1, 2)	EU	463	464	465	466	467	468	469	470
	US	305	307	310	313	316	319	322	325
	Japan	128	128	128	128	128	128	128	128
	Total	**896**	**899**	**903**	**907**	**911**	**915**	**919**	**923**
Urinary Incontinent patients (m) (3)	Men	36	36	36	36	36	37	37	37
	Women	90	90	90	91	91	91	92	92
	Total	**126**	**126**	**126**	**127**	**127**	**128**	**129**	**129**
SUI (Stress Urinary Incontinent) patients (m) (4)	Men	4	4	4	4	4	4	4	4
	Women	44	44	44	44	45	45	45	45
	Total	**48**	**48**	**48**	**48**	**49**	**49**	**49**	**49**
SUI due to muscle deficiency (m) (5)	Men	2	2	2	2	2	2	2	2
	Women	4	4	4	4	4	4	5	5
	Total	**6**	**6**	**6**	**6**	**6**	**6**	**7**	**7**
Slight and moderate cases of SUI due to muscle deficiency (m) (6)		**5**	**5**	**5**	**5.1**	**5.2**	**5.2**	**5.2**	**5.2**
Taboo factor (%) (7)		30%	30%	30%	30%	31%	32%	33%	34%
Target population (m)					1.6	1.7	1.8	1.8	1.9

(1) www.populationdata.net. Data 2005

(2) Growth rate (2005) www.indexmundi.com. Japan 0.05%; US 0.92%; EU 0.2%

(3) UI prevalence: 8% in men; 10% in women

(4) SUI prevalence: 10% in men; 49% in women

(5) SUI due to muscular deficiency: 48% in men; 10% in women

(6) Slight and moderate cases: 83% of total cases

(7) Only a proportion of patients will elect for treatment – most will keep their disease a secret – a 'taboo factor'

Figure 1.2   SUI forecast

The general structure of a term sheet is shown in Figure 1.3. A bare minimum of detail is given, around which further terms will be added to suit the needs of the parties to the transaction. These additions form the texture and colour of the transaction and can reveal the intentions and motives of the parties when viewed in the context of the market.

Therefore, it is a good idea to analyse the term sheet carefully, disentangling the motives of the other party from the legal statements. It should also be considered as an initial term sheet and an invitation to negotiate. Thus it is a valuable document. Appreciating the nuances in a term sheet often stems from previous experience and so when a proposal arrives it is useful to have it reviewed by someone with the skills to see past the words on the page. The pattern of the document can then be discerned. Pattern analysis is partly an innate skill and partly one which improves with practice and experience. A recognizable theme may emerge in the data given in a data set, a product proposition or an external pitch, which can stimulate ideas or be used to form a plan. During a presentation you may get a feeling of déjà vu and be able to apply previous experience or strategies to the case in hand. There can be a danger of stereotyping an idea as old or passé; at the same time, these echoes can help to reinforce the validity of a proposal. In investment circles the use of 'comparables' (companies with a similar profile in age, size and market sector to the target company under consideration) is formalized to the point where a 'normalized' or average model of companies in the area is used as the basis for estimating the value range of the company. Either of these approaches can be purposefully considered as a part of the analysis.

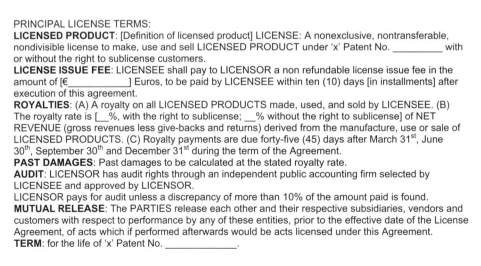

PRINCIPAL LICENSE TERMS:
LICENSED PRODUCT: [Definition of licensed product] LICENSE: A nonexclusive, nontransferable, nondivisible license to make, use and sell LICENSED PRODUCT under 'x' Patent No. _____ with or without the right to sublicense customers.
LICENSE ISSUE FEE: LICENSEE shall pay to LICENSOR a non refundable license issue fee in the amount of [€_____] Euros, to be paid by LICENSEE within ten (10) days [in installments] after execution of this agreement.
ROYALTIES: (A) A royalty on all LICENSED PRODUCTS made, used, and sold by LICENSEE. (B) The royalty rate is [__%, with the right to sublicense; __% without the right to sublicense] of NET REVENUE (gross revenues less give-backs and returns) derived from the manufacture, use or sale of LICENSED PRODUCTS. (C) Royalty payments are due forty-five (45) days after March 31st, June 30th, September 30th and December 31st during the term of the Agreement.
PAST DAMAGES: Past damages to be calculated at the stated royalty rate.
AUDIT: LICENSOR has audit rights through an independent public accounting firm selected by LICENSEE and approved by LICENSOR.
LICENSOR pays for audit unless a discrepancy of more than 10% of the amount paid is found.
MUTUAL RELEASE: The PARTIES release each other and their respective subsidiaries, vendors and customers with respect to performance by any of these entities, prior to the effective date of the License Agreement, of acts which if performed afterwards would be acts licensed under this Agreement.
TERM: for the life of 'x' Patent No. _____.

Figure 1.3   Term sheet

A good example of the use of this kind of technique came up when I was trying to find ways to increase the sales of a newly launched product which, although it had great deal of positive clinical advantages over the market leader, was not selling as well as expected. All the market research data showed that the target group of physicians seemed keen to use the product. In searching for clues to the problem nothing superficially appeared to be going wrong and so I made a fine analysis of representative calling to see if a pattern emerged. Firstly I grouped the representatives' performances into high and low sales and then I compared the activity reports of the two groups to see if they were similar or different. The best-performing reps weren't seeing more or different doctors to their colleagues, I found a pattern in their behaviour which appeared to lead to better sales. If the rep saw the pharmacist at the hospital, then the medical consultant, and then held a team meeting followed by another pharmacy call, hospital-led sales would start soon after in the region. I had a chance to present my discovery to the field force at the national sales conference and suggested that everyone should try to copy this pattern. Within 3 months our rate of growth trebled and the product really started to penetrate the market. Patterns in data, patterns in behaviour and patterns in markets are highly informative and you need to be aware of them and seek them out where possible.

NUMERICAL ANALYSIS SKILLS

There is, at least in some quarters I think, an over-reliance on the significance of 'making the numbers' which is led by practices developed in the USA. This is particularly the case when the basis for an idea is weak yet there is a kind of clarity of thought brought about by reducing the analysis to mere numbers. Statistical techniques and calculation methods will be discussed later but for the business development function numbers have the power to penetrate raw data and to persuade (or dissuade) if used judiciously. While pernickety exactitude can be a major drawback, a good 'feel' for the numbers is an essential part of the business development skill set.

HEURISTIC ANALYSIS SKILLS

Heuristic analysis is perhaps used more intuitively than consciously by most people. At its simplest it involves inferring: 'if this is true and that is true, then perhaps …' we might take this action or that, license a product or even acquire a company. Learning by doing feeds back into pattern analysis and is informative to process analysis. By invoking an heuristic approach, sometimes called 'blue-skying' or 'brainstorming', and, utilizing techniques for creative problem solving , it is possible to break out of a reductive analysis mode typically used in scientific circles which tends to produce only 'right' and 'wrong' answers. Although a reductionist approach is valuable in a great many circumstances, it can also seduce people into thinking that the alternatives are real and the only ones available. In business development as in life there is little which is so black and white and which cannot be approached from other directions.

Recently, I was advising a client who was faced with an ultimatum to either give up the shared intellectual property rights generated by their contract research, which was performed on behalf of their partner, or face non-payment of their invoices and so bankruptcy: a very stark choice. The resolution came through close examination of the legality of the threat and crucially, in the end, the place of arbitration chosen by the firm in the contract. The fact that the arbitration had to be conducted in a foreign language was very much to the research firm's advantage, and the partner was forced to compromise. Careful analysis of what seemed like a 'do it or die' ultimatum had allowed my client to prevail.

Communication

The minimum communication skills required for business development exceed those for many other specialities in business. Again I believe there are four main areas:

- linguistic
- legal
- cultural
- psychological.

LINGUISTIC COMMUNICATION

The linguistic ability of an individual is of paramount importance as it will be the basis for their reasoning. While employed as a teacher I had the experience of dealing with children whose language skills were poorly developed. Some of the characteristics they displayed can also be recognized in the population at large and even people of very high intelligence whose education has been highly specialized, for instance in science or finance, may possess only a limited vocabulary. It is the task of business development people to be able to bridge such gaps as and when they appear.

Poor linguistic ability causes particular problems where there are language differences between parties. Even the use of British English with an American-English counterparty can create misunderstandings. English is my mother tongue and this might be thought of as an advantage, yet in an international environment one can know and use too many words. In England the use of complex language is taken to indicate a high level of education and can be perceived as exclusive. In the USA, less complex forms of English are employed and this can achieve more successful communication. Speakers of English as a second language often comment to me that US speakers are 'so clear' while the British are less so. In business development there is therefore a challenge to think in complex terms, yet to communicate clearly and unambiguously. The financial consequences of business development in pharmaceuticals are so great that you need to take considerable care to express yourself as clearly as possible and to check that your intended message was the one that has been received.

LEGAL COMMUNICATION

Legal vocabulary is another minefield for the unwary in business development. When you are involved in negotiations and in contract drafting, the wrong words or the wrong construction can be costly. It is as important to avoid omissions as it is misstatements. One way to mitigate the risk is to use a checklist for each transaction and for each part of every transaction. Although, as a business development specialist, you are unlikely to have legal training, you need to be familiar with legal forms of expression and terminology; you should also understand the structure of the different kinds of transaction likely to be used. Most US states use law based on English Common Law and so have inherited some of the more bizarre terms that grew up over a thousand years of British history, even though they have no clear relevance to the current US situation so this is the place to start.

The basic building blocks of business development deals are, for the most part, contracts. These contain various degrees of complexity depending on the number of elements and parties to the contract. Partnerships and joint ventures are other legal forms with which the business developer will need to become familiar. Another part of the law which you will need to be familiar is intellectual property law which, in the pharmaceutical industry, underlies most of the value of the products. Some of the practical issues that need to be addressed by business development will be discussed in this book, but no attempt to pre-empt legal advice or interpret the legal mind will be made.

CULTURAL COMMUNICATION

Communication across cultures is another complexity to be wrestled with in the business development world. Cultural complexity may reflect national cultures, or more subtle groupings, such as academic rather than industrial scientists or manufacturing and engineering compared to marketing or finance. Each of these groups may use similar words and phrases (in the same language) and yet mean very different things. Business development need not align with any one of these groups but you should be capable of understanding and interpreting communications between the cultures within your own company and between companies where a particular cultural bias may hold sway (such as among biotech companies where scientific principle may sometimes appear to be held in higher esteem than commercial concerns). There are obvious cultural differences between private, often family-owned or family-founded companies, and public companies where a much more open style of governance is required of management. The balance between recognizing and understanding the needs of another culture with meeting the needs of your own company is a delicate one.

PSYCHOLOGICAL COMMUNICATION

The dominance of human nature over common sense is the subject of most literature and even in the context of a scientific industry (with so many otherwise rational people) there is no escaping the basic dumb instincts of humanity. A number of transactions which I've experienced have left all parties asking 'What went wrong?' after things have not gone to plan. Sometimes the problem may be hubris, the pride of a leader not wanting to be beaten; perhaps it's revenge for past losses, rivalry between old friends (often from university or business school); sometimes you could believe it's just plain deviltry. Yet, on occasion, deals are still done against logic or lost despite common sense and business development once the board has made its decision for better or worse must see it through.

Project management

One of the major skill sets for any business developer is complex project management. 'Complex' because setting a target date for completion of a negotiation is a far cry from achieving it. Using a structured yet flexible project management approach in business development can help steer any undertaking and, without usurping the decision-making role of senior management, ensure a transaction is effectively managed and value created.

As an integral part of project management, people management is a paramount skill. An intellectual understanding of a product area and the analytical skills to recognize its value are important but to move the project forward within the plan requires leadership, motivation, inducements, negotiation skills and force of personality. Measuring success in business development is a sophisticated process. The most obvious metric, deal flow (the number of completed deals), is a major part of the activity, yet of itself is inadequate. A favourite expression while at Roche was 'the licensing department's definition of a good deal is ... a deal'. Very unfair, but if rewards and bonuses are handed out on the basis of the quantity of deals there is always the risk that quality could suffer. On the other hand, when the value of a deal cannot be truly evaluated for many years where is the incentive to drive hard to get the deal done? Furthermore, value is not an absolute when considering the strategic effect of an asset acquisition on a portfolio. A product such as a diagnostic aid may only generate modest sales itself, but may be the key to incremental sales of a far more valuable product franchise. How then should the deal achievement be measured and rewarded?

Process improvement

Beyond acquisition or sale of products, there is also an opportunity to develop a business through improvements of process. These improvements might be made in distribution, procurement, document handling or any one of a number of other areas of the business where competitive status can be improved. There is no reason to exclude these from the business development remit. Indeed the overview that business development has of the process as it affects the company's ability to negotiate for and integrate new products, can be held up as an excellent mirror to the organization where problems faced in a deal may have more general implications for the company. Correcting flawed processes has significant value and should thus be attended to as the means to augment the company's development.

A good business developer should be at the centre of the business, with a 360° awareness of the influences and interactions that are part of the company. This involves sitting at the centre of an information network and enabling communication between colleagues, proactively proposing and taking action on issues, studying and predicting the competitive environment, planning and informing the board on carefully evaluated options and taking charge of the processes of change in the organization. To do all these things requires responsibility, authority and freedom of action.

Planning the Portfolio CHAPTER 2

Portfolio management

Every company can be thought of as following a broadly similar pattern to the three ages of man: birth, growth and then death. However, the company, unlike a person, can be rejuvenated even if its products fail: introduction of innovations through research and development, licensing or acquisition can bring new life to the company. New companies are started on the basis of innovative technologies and suffer all of the problems of young children. Children have no support without a parent, they are highly susceptible to diseases and accidents and in the early years are unsteady on their feet. The same is true of a fledgling company. Yet, with luck and judgement, growth can be rapid leading to significant value creation in a short period of time. When a child reaches adolescence, this rapid growth brings its own problems: finding sufficient food, clothes to wear and a role in life.

The parallel for a rapidly growing company is the need for investments in manufacturing, larger premises for administration and a broader portfolio of products. When personal maturity comes to the young person, it brings with it a steady income yet many dependants: there is a need to consolidate investments and provide for the long term. On the other hand, for the mature public company there is no option to consolidate and still provide a nearly steady income. Only by continued growth can the company maintain or increase its value. This is the imperative under which most companies are run and is the stimulus for business development activities across the board.

One of the key activities of the business development role is maintaining the portfolio of products within the company. It is therefore necessary to understand the objectives of the company and to plan accordingly. Depending on the scope of the business development role within the company, planning may also include the creation and maintenance of company strategy. Alternatively the business development person may be the agent of the strategy created by the CEO and the board. In the larger corporations business development takes on a pivotal role in both the creation and conversion of strategy into practical applications. Strategic planning as a function, therefore, should be examined in some detail.

The most common evocation of strategic planning within a company is a 5-year plan produced annually with the objective of taking a longer view than just the next year in business. This is largely a financially driven document, yet it also describes the current state of the business portfolio and, therefore, the strategic gaps which exist and must be addressed by business development. Each plan starts by looking back at the sales growth of existing products and at their forecast sales for the coming year in fine detail with projections for the following 4 years. The aggregation of the numbers from all products will describe the company's growth as a whole and so will usually be the mark by which the company's value and its share price will be judged.

The assimilation and integration of detailed information into the 5-year plan is therefore critical for decision-making regarding capital expenditure, human resource planning and promotional costs. It will also determine the need for product acquisitions, and, on a grander scale, company mergers and acquisitions.

In order to generate the background information for the 5-year plan a complete examination of the existing portfolio is required: a review of all activities which affect the conduct of the business. A number of different perspectives are required in order to describe the company's evolution to the current point. These will include activities at subsidiary level and by therapeutic area. They examine activities from the perspective of research, development, manufacturing and marketing. The company's performance will be studied intrinsically and also against competitive benchmarks: at product level, therapeutic area level and corporate level.

Evaluating the company's products

A holistic view of the company's activities is required if one is to examine each component's contribution to the business and to determine which elements are contributing the most to growth and which elements are hindering growth. The sources of information for this review are found throughout the company. Essentially a pharmaceutical company template will include inputs from the CEO, corporate finance, corporate marketing, research, development, manufacturing, supply chain, medical and regulatory, and legal and intellectual property groups. Affiliate companies will generate their own 5-year plans which will be added to the overall view. These contributions will be aggregated into an overall view of the company's potential. From a marketing perspective a now traditional method of viewing the company's products is to produce a sales and growth quadrant analysis of the portfolio and categorize the products into one of four types: cows, stars, opportunities and dogs. This is shown in Figure 2.1.

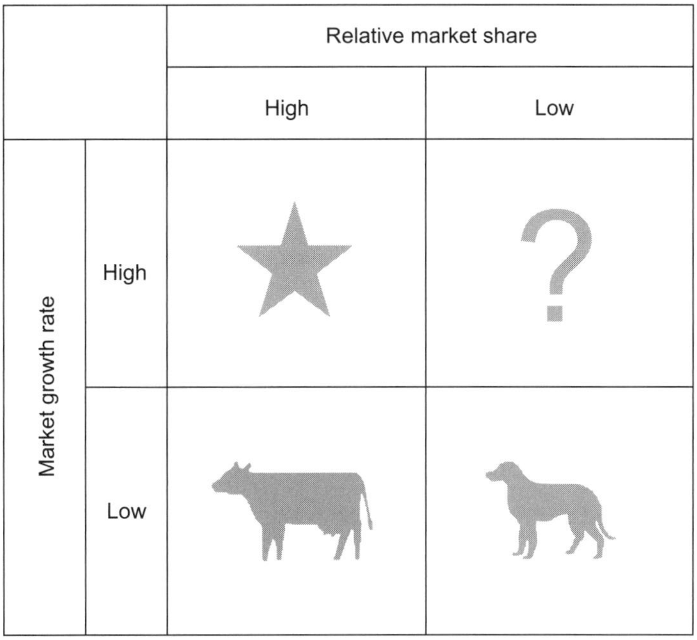

		Relative market share	
		High	Low
Market growth rate	High	★	?
	Low	🐄	🐕

Figure 2.1   Quadrant chart

The combination of high growth and high sales is the most desirable star position in the quadrant, while the low growth and low sales products are represented as dogs. The opportunities have high growth but low sales, as is typical of new products, while older products with low growth are said to be the cows for milking. Depending on the balance of the portfolio, investment would be directed towards the opportunities and stars, reduced for cows and withdrawn for dogs. This is a simple but effective analysis tool at a high level for mature companies with a broad portfolio.

It is less useful in the context of a younger company where the portfolio will tend to fall into one or two categories, leaving little strategic choice as to where to direct investment. The analysis is also restricted in its utility to marketed products. This is because development-level products and research projects have no performance to measure, only forecasts, and, understandably, the forecasts for all such projects will be good. It is therefore a good idea to take a different perspective when looking at the integrated portfolio of a larger company and to see the portfolio not only as a snapshot but as a continuum. Each project or product can be placed at a point along an axis of vintage and each cohort can be examined for the number of projects at that stage, along with their aggregate projected worth and the concentration of products in each therapeutic area. So the portfolio can be described as being weighted towards the early stage or the late stage, or perhaps as well balanced. The continuity of product supply to the market from the development portfolio is therefore a predictive factor for the company's long-term growth prospects (see Figure 2.2).

The relative strength or weakness of the company at each point in the development timeline will then be revealed. Each project's contribution to company turnover, as it comes to market and then throughout its life cycle, becomes a more relevant measure of its potential worth. The combination of products both in terms of their financial contribution and of their financial requirements will also influence the financing requirements for the company as a whole. At one phase in the strategic planning process at Roche we came to realize that the timelines for many projects brought them to market within the same 18-month period. The implications for launch costs, field-force head count and recruitment programmes were extremely serious. As a consequence we attempted to make a risk assessment of the portfolio by asking the therapeutic area teams to assign to their projects a probability of success in reaching market. Not surprisingly their view was of almost uniform success, which was not helpful to us – we needed another method for gauging risk. Rather than going to external sources regarding these sensitive issues for benchmarks and the like, the views of the ten top function heads were taken in a modification of the Delphi research method. Each was asked to rate the projects on a scale of zero to ten on probability of success. Retrospectively we were able to judge the

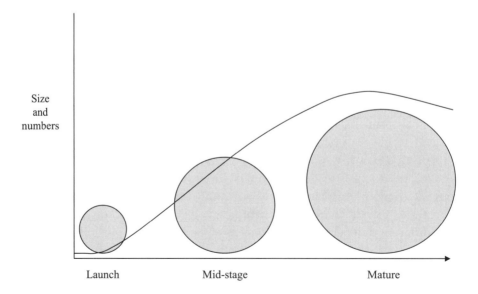

Figure 2.2   Product cohorts by vintage

value of those opinions and found them to be the most accurate guide from all our sources. While some argue that numeric analysis is preferable we became convinced that years of experience were a better arbiter.

Responding to changes in the market

In the last 10 years the impact of patent expiry on pharmaceutical products has become more significant, and this is illustrated in Figure 2.3. For innovative, research-based companies, the sophistication of the generic drug manufacturing companies has had serious consequences on revenue. Twenty years ago, when a large product lost its patent protection the main erosion of market share that it suffered would take 2 to 3 years. Now, the aggressive pursuit of abbreviated new drug applications by generic companies both in the USA and in the rest of the world can mean a major product will now lose 80 per cent of its worldwide market share in less than 3 months. No longer is there a graceful degradation in what was once a quite steady market. The more successful the patented product has been, the greater the loss.

This phenomenon has had a dramatic effect on strategic planning within large pharmaceutical companies. The resulting abrupt removal of several billion dollars in annual profits makes the maintenance of a strong research and development portfolio absolutely vital. Much has been written by equity analysts over the years about the relative strengths or weaknesses of companies'

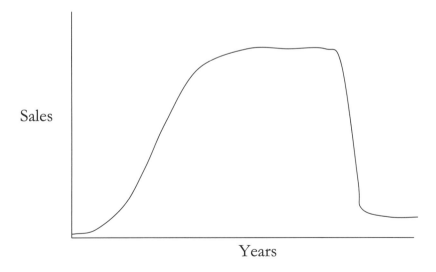

Figure 2.3   Patent expiry

portfolios, yet none of the larger companies has been able to demonstrate an adequate flow of new large products from its own research. The natural consequence of this has been an ever upward trend towards in-licensing of products. Looked at simply, if you have $10 billion in sales, then each year you must add another billion dollars in sales if you are to produce double-digit growth. The consolidation of the industry over the last 10 years has meant that corporations are now much larger than this and annual growth requirements may be as much as $5 billion. Combining these figures with an equal drop in revenues through patent expiries can mean a requirement to produce far more. Hence it is a safe prediction the company acquisitions will continue apace and that in-licensing will continue to dominate the market as the means to generate corporate growth.

Nevertheless, internal research and development programmes continue to be a mainstay of expenditure among the larger organizations. However, this is risky: estimates of the success rate in drug discovery produce a picture of massive failure (see Figure 2.4).

The number of chemical compounds which are potential drug candidates and which will need to be screened for activity in order to generate a possible compound will be in the tens of thousands. In former times it took many years to achieve success in this area and there was a low yield per thousand candidates. Today, despite new and massively automated screening techniques, there has been no significant increase in the number of candidates with the potential to become a drug. Even automated screening techniques have not significantly increased the number of candidates with the magical potential to become a

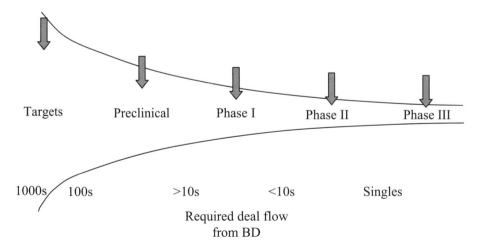

Figure 2.4   Discovery success

drug. The confluence of attributes which constitute a molecule that is both safe and efficacious is a rare event. Rarer still is a molecule which has these characteristics and will prove better than existing therapies. Furthermore the advances in diagnostic analytical techniques have revealed a great many more adverse events which compounds in development must avoid. As a result the regulatory hurdle for products has risen progressively. The corollary of this is that companies are much more cautious about investing in their research-level compounds unless and until they can demonstrate a level of safety far beyond previous standards. As the cost of bringing a product to market is now estimated to be as much as $800 million, if the product is unlikely to be able to address a wide market the cost of development is prohibitive. It therefore makes sense for companies to invest in products which have already been developed to a stage where the safety has been established. Once again this sets the stage for a vastly increased focus on in-licensing. The larger pharma companies are now locked in a battle not only for market share but also for privileged access to the early stage compounds which will form the products of tomorrow. While this trend is probably unsustainable in the long term, at the moment none of the larger players can afford to back off and allow the others free access.

Incorporating products at the development level permits a leavening of the portfolio mix and a reinforcement of weaknesses in portfolio strength. It also guards against attrition of one's own products' failure to progress to market due to scientific risks. The objective of strategic planning therefore is to achieve an optimum balance of investment in internal research and external acquisitions to justify investors' confidence, by demonstrating a continued ability to generate strong growth in a highly competitive market. As the capital base of each company expands so the demands to provide a competitive return on investment and earnings per share will increase. It is only by demonstrating a solid business plan that investors' confidence can be gained and retained. Failing that the only remaining route for a company is merger or acquisition (see Figure 2.5).

Balancing the portfolio

In evaluating the planning dimensions that must be considered in order to balance a portfolio three major areas should be played off one against the other. These are:

- life-cycle management
- development and
- overall portfolio balance.

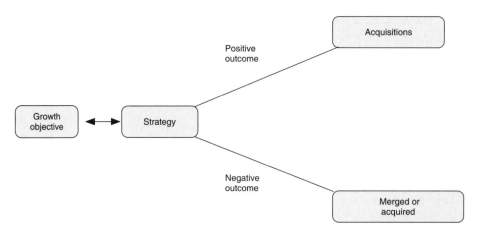

Figure 2.5   Mergers and acquisitions

None of these is independent of the other: products may be brought into development along the timeline of vintages; these may be inserted into one or more therapeutic areas and matched for their profit or market size. Major brands can be reinforced by life-cycle management initiatives including new formulations to extend the main franchise, different forms to suit a wider catchment of patients and the extension to new indications possibly by the use of different or novel formulations at the same time.

There are, however, increasing pressures on simple life-cycle enhancements by formulation changes. Recent work by Hans Dettmers of Novartis has shown that of all the patent applications for new formulations of older products made in the last 5 years, 80 per cent have faced patent oppositions – all from generic manufacturers trying to prevent the extension of the main brand franchise (see Figure 2.6). In fact as few as 25 per cent of the applications filed have actually been granted at all and most of these have been changed to some degree with narrower claims or reduced scope.

This restriction to the freedom of companies with original intellectual property (IP) is rarely heard about yet it highlights the continual need for new compounds as a source of growth, in addition to extensions to the life of existing products. The chief means of supplementing a company's own research and development thus remains the in-licensing or acquisition of products through business development. Indeed much business research has shown that the growth of the top companies has been largely due to their ability to acquire products in these ways, to develop them and to bring them to market. Specialty companies, such as Forest, Shire and Reliant, have since been built entirely from these sources and are forces to be reckoned with in the marketplace.

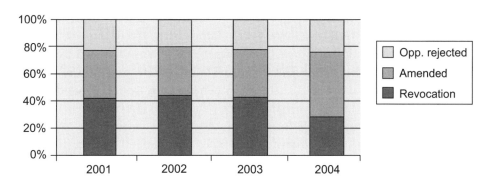

Figure 2.6   A61k patent oppositions

Balancing the portfolio by the inclusion of in-licensed compounds can be more expensive and deliver less profit in the long term, yet the reduction in risk associated with in-licensing counterbalances these shortcomings. Overall the portfolio represents both the supply side of the company's innovations and the demand side through the gaps that open up between its own products in time, size and profitability. Whether the business development department is the strategic planning department or works closely with a separate function, the integration of this plan creates the motivation for in-licensing acquisition and divestments. Continuous analysis of the marketplace including competitive intelligence, market research and benchmarking of the company's performance as a business will provide a backdrop to the company's competitive status and relative attraction to the capital markets. The value placed on the company's shares will dictate its ability to borrow money at a given rate. The more secure the company's earnings appear, the more confidence investors will have and this will be reflected in the company's cost of capital. The cost of capital then becomes the internal hurdle against which projects must be judged for inclusion in the portfolio as it will be one of the reference points for the discount rate applied to licensing transactions. In the network of risks and rewards the financial hurdle will always be present yet, as it is observed in many financial textbooks, return on investment is typically far higher in the long term when invested in operational businesses compared to financial instruments. The risk is much higher but then so must be the rewards.

In the pharmaceutical industry large profit margins have been justified by the risks the industry undertakes. The ever-increasing estimates of the costs of drug development are testimony to the concentration of risk on individual products. The probabilities of a novel pharmaceutical compound succeeding are very small indeed. The complexities of human biology allied to the genetic variability of patients and the range of ages, states of nutrition and status of their immune systems argue against the possibility of a universally safe and effective pharmaceutical medicine. As regulatory agencies become less tolerant of risk, the chances of finding such a therapeutic agent are reduced. An era of individualized medicine brought about by the exquisite precision of current diagnostic methods would be welcomed by clinicians yet would demand radical change in the pharmaceutical marketplace. The economies of scale achievable through the discovery of a blockbuster drug would be lost and with that extraordinary levels of funding which are currently applied to drug discovery and development. Without these levels of investment the means to provide adequate data to support regulatory submissions would disappear. Recent history has shown that in the first-world products delivering an extension of life in what is called catastrophic care situations will be afforded by those who can pay. The continued development of such medicines would therefore seem to require an imbalance in the market where innovations are paid for by the few in the short term with an extension to a broader population following patent expiry. There is an impatience with this system yet no other adequate model has been proposed as a substitute for it.

The portfolio of a company will therefore always be a compromise between short-term pressures and long-term objectives. For smaller companies short-term pressures will remain the primary focus as the main commercial objective is to attract sufficient funds to continue the development of the products in the portfolio. For the largest companies long-term planning must form a significant part of their platform. In between, companies have a choice: to concentrate on short-term measures and focus their business model or to diversify and play a longer game. Publicly traded companies have fewer options than those which are privately held as they must compete for funds with companies from other sectors. Privately held companies have the relative luxury, once they are cash positive, of choosing the direction and timescale of their development; however, the speed of change in the market has unsettled a number of traditionally privately held companies to the point where their founders have sold their stakes and exited the industry.

There are several clear trends emerging in the world market but as yet these are not convergent. Indeed some of the trends can appear to be mutually exclusive. As a result portfolio choices have never been more difficult. It seems likely that the markets will remain turbulent but the demand for improved health care across the globe will remain insatiable. It remains to be seen at what cost this demand can be satisfied and whether a company having a mixed portfolio will be more sustainable though generating lower growth or if a concentrated portfolio of specialist products being continually supplanted through constant innovation can be maintained in the long term. The choices for top company CEOs are few, yet with a planning timeframe in tens of years compared with employment tenures of 5 years or fewer, it is possible to imagine that short-term objectives may override long-term concerns.

Identifying the Needs   CHAPTER

3

I received an email this morning from a client who has been asked to provide information on potential takeover targets for his company and he asked me how they might go about such a transaction. Their target price was in the range of $50–100 million. While this is not be an unusual request for an adviser in M&A to receive, when it is put to someone in business development a series of questions about just why and how the company has made this decision is raised. In order to understand the background to such a request the structures, processes and practices of business development in different company situations needs some examination.

Many of the largest companies have business development departments which are split into three main functions. These are:

- search and evaluation

- negotiation

- alliance management.

I shall come to look at each of these broad headings in turn, but in the first instance it is ultimately necessary to establish why you want to search and, not surprisingly, for what. If the search is for a product the approach would be different to that taken to find a partner for a research programme, and different again if seeking to make a takeover. In order to choose any one of these as the best way to improve the business and take the appropriate path a review of the pressures and opportunities the company is facing must be completed. In order to achieve this you will need a method, a 'what to do' to improve the business. So there is a need to look at the current situation of the business, to make some judgement about its worth and its direction and whether or not to do something about it. Only then can you come to the decision about what should be done and how. The primary issues concerning any business relate to its state of health, considered in each of its parts and as a whole. In other words, is it fit for the job? Then, if one is somewhat philosophical in nature, perhaps one might ask: 'What is the overall purpose of the business?'

This brings me to probably the most basic (but often forgotten) trio of management fundamentals: objectives, strategy and tactics.

Objectives are on the horizon, strategy is the starting point and tactics are the steps on the way. The indiscriminate use of these words is perhaps one of the more challenging issues in business development as the terms are so often used synonymously. If an objective is not known and not clear, then no strategy will have a point and any tactics will be far more likely to do harm than good. If the business development function can bring discipline, in terms of understanding and using these words, to the organization in which it operates, then much will have been achieved. One of the best ways to distinguish between these terms is to define them simply. An *objective* might be to go to London; this objective then might be modified by such words as 'fast', 'in luxury' or 'most economically'. A *strategy* can then be chosen to suit the selected objective. One might go by train, plane, car, barge, bicycle, walk or any number of other alternatives and then *tactically* one can choose to travel early, midday, late, or overnight. The objective is clear – to go to London – the strategy dictates how and then the tactical choices become clear.

In business the word 'objective' is often not used so explicitly. For instance the business objectives of a 5-year plan can sometimes seem to fall foul of

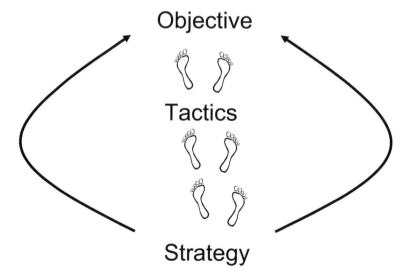

Figure 3.1   Objectives, strategy and tactics

the sort of 'mission statement' which calls for 'leadership' in perhaps social responsibility or some such phrase, whereas an objective is a definite and measurable thing, not a loosely phrased ambition. To my mind there should be no such opportunity for confusion in the objectives of a business if they are thought through and articulated properly.

The old and well-tried SMART acronym (Specific, Measurable, Achievable, Realistic and Timed), when applied to objective setting, allows little latitude for flowery speech and is therefore an excellent axiom for business development to stand by. First, an objective must be specific. For example, if you state your objective as being 'market leader' – or worse 'a market leader' – this has almost no meaning. On the other hand, if you state it as becoming the clear market leader by a stated percentage of market share, this is specific. It is also measurable: the second of the tenets of a SMART objective. Introducing a metric, like this, makes it possible to reveal the nature of the objective in relation to competitors or previous performance. However, a metric is not enough: market leadership might be achieved but for only a single day. The 'T' in SMART signifies time: the objective must be reached for a specified period of time and also by a particular date (for how long and by when).

The other major elements of SMART are the 'A' and the 'R': achievability and realism. These really are the test of a management's ambition and resolve, yet also of its compassion and honesty. Managements need to set ambitious targets for themselves and their teams, yet these targets must be grounded in reality; shooting for the moon is not possible without the resources and opportunity to get there. While sometimes a target that really stretches capability can bring a result which is greater than either management or staff initially believed they might achieve, at the same time if the goal is set so high that it is unattainable it becomes a disincentive to trying. Achievability as a theoretical concept can be hard to quantify beyond a certain threshold, because the only way to test it is to try it; even so some goals are plainly out of reach either due to the capacity of a market to change either over time or because of saturation of the available customers. In declaring an objective therefore one must guard against over-optimism. There is a fine line between success and failure and at times it is prudent to under-promise and over-deliver. Consequently an adage I carry in my mind always is, in my opinion, 'the true definition of a failure' and that is: 'A man who aims low, and misses'.

So a SMART objective is the cutting edge for business development. It allows you to separate empty words from hard, clear decisions. It helps to keep your feet on the ground and to be honest in, and to, your ambitions. For the business, setting objectives and understanding them helps to refine the rest of the organization's activities towards the best outcome. 'SMART' is a way to think clearly about *where* you are going and *what* it's worth. In practice the differences between a big business and a small one are slight, but in big companies an individual may perceive themselves as having no volition or free will: the organization and its history have such momentum that a single person can have little impact. In a small company the opposite can appear true and it can seem that every decision, every action, can have an immediate and dire consequence. Having worked in both circumstances and in several places in-between, I've had some excellent tutors who helped in dealing with these perceptions. At Roche I was privileged to be in at the beginning of a number of initiatives (which since have borne fruit). At the time when an idea comes to you, seemingly alone, amongst 50,000 other employees, it seems hard to believe that idea could be made to take root. Yet if you put ideas forward it will not be long before colleagues either respond to a good idea or reject a bad one. Naturally good ideas rarely have only one origin: in fact most only take root because many people have drawn the same conclusions more or less simultaneously and someone must speak out for change. Business development can therefore act as a lens to focus ideas and to articulate them on behalf of the business. I've frequently been wrong over the years by backing what seemed a good idea only to have it (correctly) shot down by my colleagues. Yet these instances are rapidly forgotten and even if one gains a reputation for being adventurous there has to be someone in the organization, and it is not so strange that the better idea an idea is, the sooner it somehow become someone else's great idea! The job of business development in these situations is to somehow advance all that seems good, take the laughter when it's wrong and perhaps share some of the credit when success arrives. That at least in a big business can bring success.

By contrast, in a small business as the relationship between the decision, statement and action are relatively short it can feel like everything is out of control and that experimentation is dangerous. While up to a point this may be true, with hindsight many of these decisions become quite trivial. As Bill Burns, CEO of Roche Pharmaceuticals, often says, 'Everything has its rhythm' and Brian Moyse, former marketing manager at G.D. Searle in the UK, used to tell me many years ago: 'Let's wait a bit.' Bill and Brian, with the benefit of many years of experience, were both saying: be prepared to let time take care of the crisis and guess what, quite often it does. In the world of business development often every day has its crises, and there is always pressure to perform, yet even when the size of the organization is taken into account speed is not usually crucial, particularly when it comes to taking action. In theory the bigger the relative importance of a decision, the more considered it ought to be. Despite the apparent urgency of some decisions they can often wait.

In sum, if the objective is clear this can be informative for every subsequent decision in the business. When faced with a choice between one alternative and another at a strategic or tactical level the clarity of the objective and the way it is articulated are of the greatest importance.

Portfolio objectives

Let us return to the colleague who e-mailed me this morning about providing information on potential takeover targets for his company. He had framed his question to me wrongly and, without knowing his company's objective behind the takeover it was difficult to give any useful advice. So what is the objective? Has his company suffered a setback and is it being forced to make changes? Does it lack for opportunities in its home market? Are its competitive status or pricing not attractive in its locality? Were its products old and unattractive? Maybe the company sought a takeover because the targets were in new and demanding markets and partnering or licensing would not be sufficient? Pretty much all companies' objectives stem from one of these situations and this is why I term the opening gambit for assessment a 'situation analysis'.

Every company's business situation will be an amalgam of its portfolio, its finances, and the management and operational strengths. A cross-analysis of these elements can be summed up as the strengths and weaknesses of the organization, the company's internal attributes. These attributes can be contrasted against each other, and expressed as: 'This is either done well or badly in or by the company' in an empirical assessment. It is also possible to gain some view of best practices within and between industries by means of benchmarking studies of other similar companies. However, benchmarking is only useful when the organization has a clear assessment of its own resources. In other words if you think something in the company is poor anyway, knowing that competitors are better or worse doesn't help.

An evaluation of the company's functional capability to execute its plans will be the basis for deciding if an objective is currently achievable and realistic. If this is not the case changes to the organization will be required in order to meet the objective. The relationship between the internal landscape of strengths and weaknesses and the chosen objective will thus be one of the key considerations in setting the objective. When a company is small or has a limited geographic scope it will not have the resources to undertake a multinational product launch on its own. Yet this does not prevent it declaring this as a valid objective if it opts to partner its product with a bigger company. It will, however, have to give up pretensions of being the 'leader' in this case.

The other side of the situation analysis though is the real world. Here, competitors will be moving independently of the company's internal concerns and it is by looking at the activities of these competitors and at the market itself that opportunities will be revealed. The results of the company's performance must generate improvements in turnover or profit for its shareholders, but to remain attractive as a continuing investment these improvements will also need to be reflected in comparable or better growth than national or international competitors.

Quantifying SWOT

Normally it is the role of the business development function to monitor and take action to ensure growth through the acquisition of assets; occasionally the best interests of the shareholders will be served by an exit and a sale of assets or even of the company. However, for the purposes of this text it will usually be assumed that the situation analysis indicates that opportunities exist and the business has the necessary strengths to address them. Following this assumption, the remaining players in this drama are the markets themselves for they are both the actors and the stage. This may be at the level of market of customers for products, markets of competitors or markets for stock in companies vying for investment to exploit their opportunities. The movements of markets can be seen as being independent of a company's actions or responsive to them. Customers will respond favourably to products by purchasing them, competitors will move to counter each others' promotions and investors will make choices of where to put their money. The situation analysis also needs to include the current trends in customer acceptance, competitive activities and stock market trends. These external influences represent the Opportunities and Threats which a company must address and overcome to succeed. Between the internal and external influences lies the opportunity of profit and contrasting the elements of these dimensions is often referred to as a SWOT analysis (see Figure 3.2). The Strengths, Weaknesses, Opportunities and Threats are the cardinal points on the map of the company's situation analysis at a single point in time and will define its potential in relation to its objectives. Calibrating the relative merits of each of these elements reveals not only the current state of play for the business but its potential for change; for every threat there is an opportunity and for every weakness a need to strengthen it. Yet to make this analysis requires a method to standardize the assessment of what can be very different influences. A method I have adopted successfully in business planning and business development arises from my time in Marketing Improvements Ltd where a technique we knew as a Numerical SWOT was developed to assist in discriminating market segments for the enhancement of product marketing plans. Making suitable amendments for the purposes of business development the method is equally applicable to the situation analysis and can help in the selection of appropriate opportunities for acquisitions and licensing in pharmaceutical markets.

The method is simple and yet sophisticated enough to render a visual representation of the result not seen in the traditional listed results of a SWOT.

In the numerical version each of the variables is assigned to one of the two scales, Strength and Weakness or Opportunity and Threat – and given a ranking and a weighting. This would not work if the variables in the description remained contrary to one another. In order to standardize the inputs in a way which can be represented clearly in a graphical form all the attributes with any negative connotation and the weaknesses and the threats are reworded. For instance, if your clinical trial results are not strong, instead of writing, 'Weak clinical trials' you would write, 'Strong clinical trials'. You might also evaluate this attribute to be the most important for the success of a product, in which case it would be ranked at No. 1 of all the strengths and weaknesses. In order to differentiate how much more important this attribute is, all of the attributes

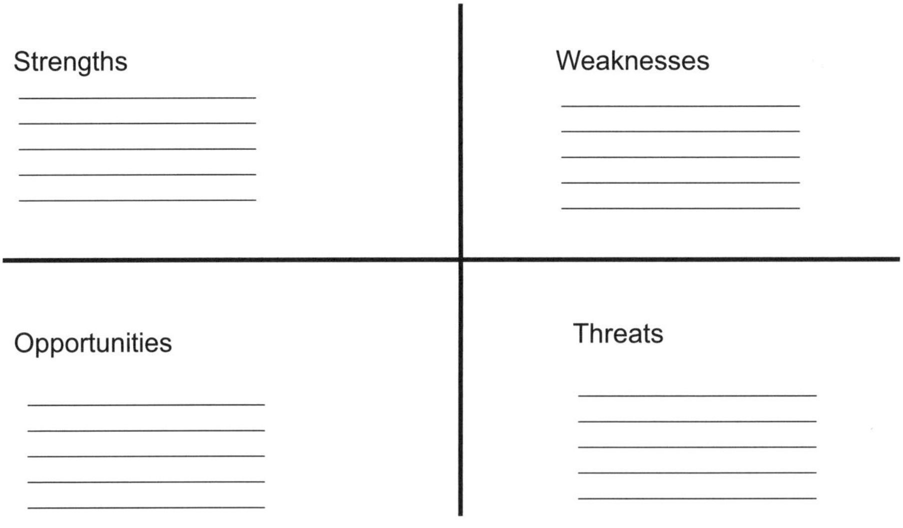

Strengths

Weaknesses

Opportunities

Threats

Figure 3.2   Traditional SWOT

will be allocated points from a total of 100 to show a relative weighting. In this case it might be 30 points out of 100 and would be the most significant attribute. Yet we know that originally the clinical trial attribute was a weakness so, to restore the balance, the attributes which make up a strong opportunity for this product are given a negative score. The range of scores runs from -1 for negative attributes through 0 (zero) where the attribute is important but the attribute is neutral in this respect through a range of positive scores from +1 to +3. In this way the SWOT can describe the ideal attributes for an Opportunity or Strength and then, through the scoring mechanism, describe how closely and in what respects an Opportunity fits the bill and how and where it differs from others under evaluation. In this case where strong clinical trial results are very important a negative score would almost certainly lead to the opportunity being dismissed if other products score positively (see Figure 3.3).

Figures 3.4 and 3.5 show two possible in-licensing opportunities and how the method can reveal the 'fit' of each to the internal landscape or the relative merits with regard to the marketplace and be plotted against each other and a quadrant chart produced to visualize the result.

The advantage of visualizing the results is that the significance of the attributes which define the opportunity can be drawn out. If the product is strong but the market is weak or massively competitive the ability (and willingness) of the company to take up the challenge can be tested. Moreover,

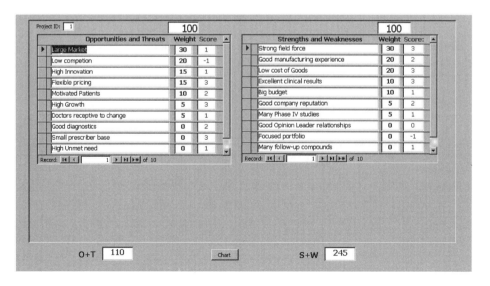

Figure 3.3   Numerical SWOT components

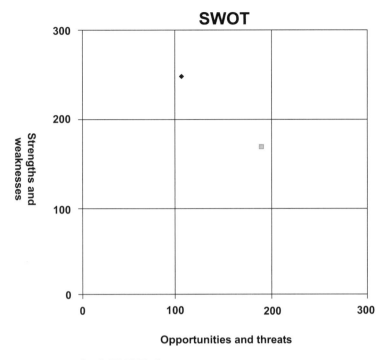

Figure 3.4   Numerical SWOT chart

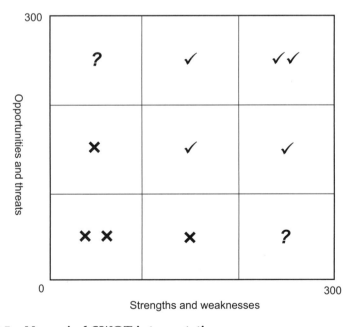

Figure 3.5   Numerical SWOT interpretation

because the contributing factors, the attributes, have been identified and quantitatively differentiated, a plan can be made to address internal shortfalls if it is believed that the market opportunity exists and is of sufficient comparative worth to others be they internal or external to the company. By cross-casting different scenarios in relation to business development opportunities, the relative attraction of an opportunity can be gauged as well as the achievability or realism. This approach can even be adapted to assessments of projected business plan outcomes in different scenarios and so can be used to determine the better of different alternatives. Where a situation could be more attractive if a change were made to the business, such as increasing the field force or in-house manufacturing, then an alteration to the business can be put in hand. In other words the lists created to demonstrate the SWOT become a diagnostic for how to improve the business both internally and externally. Modifying the internal landscape can enhance existing products and/or external opportunities can enable a much enhanced performance from the existing organization.

By using this discriminative tool it is possible to build up landscapes of positive and negative attributes which will reveal the gaps between the current situation and a desired objective. From this can come the menu of opportunities which business development can seek in the marketplace, in other words the strategic alternatives.

Locating gaps

But before business development sets out to go shopping a closer idea of the requirements is needed. Each market can be thought of as being a landscape, populated with competitors and customers in varying states of strength and activity. This becomes the environment in which a product must exist and survive. The perception of any product will be affected by its environment so, depending on the context, the same opportunity might look better or worse. While it isn't always possible to achieve an ideal it is nevertheless necessary to know the relative attraction of the available products to establish an idea of their value. Just the other day I was approached by a company 'on the product acquisition trail' who had discovered a licence opportunity which was marketed in Europe and which was apparently available for the US market. The product claimed to act as a disease modifying agent for osteoarthritis; moreover this was achieved through a recognized mechanism of action (this sort of information is of major importance to most major pharmaceutical companies). Because the product had been on the market in the EU for some years it had proven safety data and tested manufacturing methods and, according to the owner, much of the preclinical work would be acceptable to the FDA. It sounded ideal to the

US company but a quick look at the clinical data available from the existing markets revealed that while the product did actually have the claimed disease modifying effect, unfortunately at the best-tolerated dose the effect was so slight that there was no benefit over any standard therapy. Thus despite the package, the history and the superficial attraction I strongly advised the company not to pay the $20 million upfront access fee which was being demanded, never mind the following $30 million in milestone payments they were asking and the further $50 million required in clinical development costs. Even then it would not be sure of gaining market approval! In addition, the product would have needed strong marketing to achieve enough market share to pay back this level of investment cost and this was well beyond the client's funding capability. In this case although the description was right – if misleading – the price was very wrong and so was the clinical effectiveness. Altogether therefore each product needs to meet the complete profile for the market and the company.

Gap analysis

In order to make best use of the situation analysis from a strategic perspective it is wise to look not just for opportunities that are currently exploited but also for those which have yet to be addressed in the marketplace. 'Clarior e tenebris' is the Latin phrase meaning roughly 'Clearer from the darkness', which indicates that the obvious or superficial evidence from a set of data may not tell the whole, or even the correct story. In a market analysis it is often the silhouette of an opportunity which reveals its underlying value rather than a direct view. To be useful in a systematic approach this method needs to be codified in a manner which helps business development both to see and show others where opportunities lie beyond and between the obviously exploited areas. This is often referred to as a 'gap analysis', during which an examination of the marketplace is conducted first from one perspective and then from another. These two views may then be compared and the resulting combinations or subtractions can show areas which may be of potential interest. These areas must of course still obey the rules for being Achievable and Realistic and these, to a large extent, be determined by choices made in the selection of parameters for the analysis. Loose definitions usually lead to loose analyses and a lack of clarity gives an impaired ability to address the opportunity even where one is identified. Using the criteria of Measurability, Timing and Specificity, in this case a tightness of definition, is again SMART when allied to the other two criteria, so this reversal of the definition can bring a penetrating view to the process of analyzing the market. Thinking graphically, the first two axes in such a multidimensional analysis are the (closely defined) market size and the market growth. In order to give some elaboration to the market view this may also be broken down by product or if a functional or need-based segmentation has been identified in the market which overarches the product definitions this can sometimes be illustrated through such techniques as factoring and clustering which are often used in statistical analysis of large data sets to reveal patterns not seen by looking at the raw data.

In health care the existence of a number of different sources of high quality and detailed quantitative market data for such analyses confers an advantage over many other industrial markets. This is not so in many other business markets, such as chemicals or other commodities, and is more akin to consumer market data. Hence it is possible to generate analysis of data at a high level of granularity at a quantitative level rather than having to rely on qualitative research based only on small samples of the market for the estimation of segments or, of product use.

The initial analysis is frequently represented in chart form to highlight salient features such as growth versus size, where segments may be represented by circles and with each product's market share shown within (see Figure 3.6).

In such a diagram it is then possible to see the relative value of one sector versus another as well as the share each product takes of each segment and thus its respective power in each segment. By these means it is possible to see that

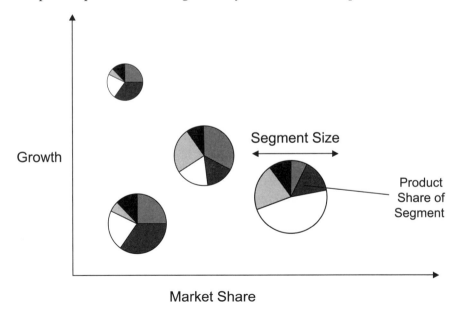

Figure 3.6   Growth circles

while a segment may look attractive from the point of view of size it may be poor from the point of view of growth. It might also be dominated by a product from a single large manufacturer. This may then lead to an examination of the competitive landscape within the segment. It could be that a large segment dominated by a powerful leader may be thought unattractive if that leader's product is relatively new and receiving strong marketing support. Conversely, if the product is old it may be about to suffer generic substitution resulting in a collapse of the segment's cash value (even though the sales volume would persist). However, if your own product has sufficient functional advantages over such a product or situation neither of these constraints may prove to be a barrier.

Functional advantages

A good example is the prescription use of Prilosec, branded ompeprazole and once the largest product in the USA, versus Zantac, branded ranitidine and the largest product by sales value. When the Zantac patent was about to expire there was considerable speculation that generic forms of ranitidine would stop the growth of Prilosec by providing an effective and cheap form of ulcer therapy. In the event, Prilosec's growth was not only undiminished in the ulcer segment but accelerated by the addition of an approval for GERD (Gastroesophageal Reflux Disease, sometimes known as Acid Reflux), which became a new segment. Although Prilosec was sold at a premium price over both Zantac and generic ranitidine, it had a functional advantage over Zantac – Prilosec relieves ulcer pain sooner after the start of therapy than ranitidine. Thus US physicians found it nearly impossible to persuade patients to change to a cheaper form (even though this mitigates the cost to the patient).

This kind of insight into the dynamics of a market is important in identifying underlying features which may contradict what would otherwise be a logical conclusion. In this case a well-known and effective product, available at a much cheaper price, would logically be an attractive alternative for patients. Market research conducted at the time clearly showed, however, that patient behaviour would overcome 'natural' logic. Here again it is the role of business development to look at opportunities at a more than superficial level and develop scenarios for potential future markets which include social and contextual influences. It is worth noting though that some trends are 'climatic' (such as the increase in market size due to increasing population) and therefore cannot be changed by a company while others can be considered as 'weather' (to be short lived) and in these cases the company might take avoiding action or take advantage of the situation. However, the health care market is increasingly a consumer-driven one, and as a result other trends are emerging that can be enhanced or even stimulated by the industry by means of promotion. There have been claims made of late that certain diseases, such as Attention Deficit Hyperactivity Disorder, and some other social and psychological phenomena have been exaggerated or invented by the pharmaceutical industry to generate an unwarranted number of prescriptions. Such practices would be avoided by the industry especially if the motive were to 'invent' disorders solely as a means to increase profits. There is ample real and serious disease which deserves the investment of time and money to serve that purpose. Furthermore the pharmaceutical industry is also generally unlikely to gratuitously feed such ammunition to its critics unless there is a sufficient medical demand for such therapies.

The facts of the matter are that physicians have turned to pharmaceutical products in an attempt to provide symptomatic relief for their patients' problems based on observations of patients receiving the products in other situations. The companies involved have responded by undertaking the clinical trials needed to prove the benefit and gain approval for these products so responding to a market need.

The discovery of true medical needs by retrospective analysis of data has been demonstrated clearly. Minocyclin is an example of a drug subjected to such an analysis, which brought about a new product. It had been noted that although minocyclin was originally developed as a broad spectrum injectable antibiotic with use in diseases such as anthrax and cholera, acne responds well to low doses of the oral form of the product. It was therefore reformulated specifically for acne and marketed for adolescent acne, particularly for girls. The resulting improvement in spots also brought about an improvement in self-esteem and this, doctors noted, reduced the need for antidepressants and other medicines. Indeed, the prospective treatment of essential benign hypertension for the prevention of coronary artery disease remained an unproven theory for many years before epidemiological data collected over the last 20 years demonstrated that this specific intervention has brought about major risk reduction of heart attacks (when combined with other risk factor reductions) and that this was particularly so when introduced early in treatment. Yet I remember well many publications offering criticism of the practice of treating mildly raised blood pressure and citing it as an invention of the pharmaceutical industry and merely for profit. In fact at the end of the 1980s many UK doctors declared that diuretics and beta blockers (newly available as cheap generics) were perfectly adequate treatment and that research into new agents was a waste of money which would be better spent on more relevant diseases such as malaria. While malaria has had less attention than one would like, the advent of ACE inhibitors and Co-enzyme A inhibitors – and their recent adoption as the new 'best practice' in the treatment of hypertension and so the reduction in the incidence of heart disease – acts as clear witness to the value of farsighted analysis of the functional needs of the market. These will often show the shortfalls of existing therapies and reveal the gap which needs to be filled which can encourage scientists if they believe they can deliver a better result from a new target elsewhere in the treatment pathway.

Segmentation

There are several ways of reflecting segmentation which can be helpful to business development analysis. One is the classic organization chart (see Figure 3.7), an approach which represents the segments each as a daughter set of a larger group.

This is perfectly reasonable if there is a clear relationship and differentiation of features between the segments in question. In an analysis of pharmaceutical functions or of anatomy, for instance, using these descriptions as group terms is quite logical when based on the needs of the market (defined as patients suffering from a particular disease or of the physical functions of a product). These groupings benefit from being able to define *how many* patients exist or *how much* product has been used according to the definitions used. This classic approach is less effective where quantification is difficult or differentiation is weak. To take a non-health-care subject, washing powders may be segmented, as in Figure 3.8, where a physical description of the products can be differentiated and then, by use of qualitative research, estimates of the numbers of customers who use the products in a different manner can be made.

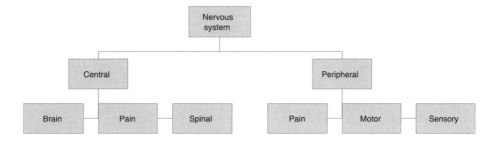

Figure 3.7   CNS organization chart

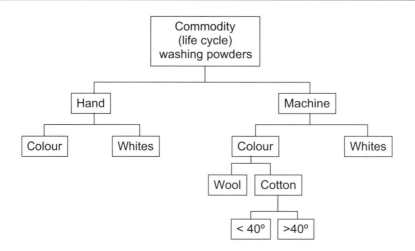

Figure 3.8   Market segmentation by product function: a gap analysis

A sample of 1000 house-persons, stratified by socioeconomic class and geography, can then act as a model of the washing powder market; it can be extrapolated to the whole population by mapping the sample to the country's census data.

In pharmaceutical markets segment analysis can be more complex for, despite the existence of fairly comprehensive data on the incidence, prevalence and treatment patterns of diseases among patients, there are, even so, problems of definition. Drugs by their very nature are often effective for more than one disease as they work on mechanisms in the body which are involved in the genesis of many diseases. As a result segmentation based on the active pharmaceutical ingredient may be misleading since it ignores these functional differences. Segmentation by disease too can be effective as a marketing tool when used prospectively as in 'drugs used to treat high blood pressure' but can be hard to measure in practical terms. For instance, a drug used for hypertension may produce its effect pharmacologically through vasodilatation; this action may also make the drug useful for diseases such as Reynaud's syndrome, where peripheral blood vessels go into spasm and cause painful local blood loss in fingers or hands, or in congestive heart failure, by reducing the 'afterload' on the heart (or the central blood pressure the heart must beat against) and this can confound useful analysis.

Portfolio constraints

This brings the question: by which segment or segments should the drug be assessed? Each of these segments will have its own dynamics and so will be more or less penetrable and more or less rewarding. The number of patients in each will be different as will the benefits of treatment and so will have a different potential value. Consequently although a drug overall may have many segmental opportunities, the inequality of these opportunities should lead to a great many segments being discounted for purposes of evaluation.

Thus, rather than using a classical approach as a standard method, it is quite often necessary to take a multidimensional view of a product's potential by assessing the various definitional possibilities. The objective here is to seek the best opportunity and this is made up of the combination of the product and its market. A superb product in an impenetrable market will have less attraction than an adequate product in an easier market from an economic perspective. Indeed, much of the proliferation of so-called 'me-too' products, which companies prefer to developing products for small indications (or specified uses for drugs), stems from this economic imperative. A great many companies are induced to market line extensions and fast-follower copies with little real functional difference because the economic results will subsidize research into innovative but less frequently found compounds. Choosing the segmentation method by looking for the best fit to the market assists business development in its understanding of the opportunity. It will also help to identify the issues that must be overcome to be successful in clinical development and then marketing. Business plans for products must consistently survive the tests of being Achievable and Realistic to be worth pursuing.

The antibiotic markets are a wonderful example of segmentation at work. The functions of an antibiotic are well defined by the bacteria they kill and these themselves are sub-divided by their own characteristics, such as pathogenicity, aerobic or anaerobic respiration, susceptibility to antibiotic types and so on. Products in development today are selected for their segmental and cross-segmental functions which are known to confer value in the marketplace. The design of the clinical trials made to demonstrate their functions are an exquisite expression of the use of market segmentation driving drug development.

This brings us to the question of how to look for a product opportunity in business development and in particular where to start. This will necessarily also be partly a function of company history, after all it is rare to be given a completely blank sheet to build a business.

An internal review is thus advisable although this should be conducted in the knowledge that it ought not to exclude consideration of new product areas, it is just that the relative attraction of some areas will become a higher when there is a harmony between internal resources and the product opportunity. The key parameters they should be considering are:

- *Size*: geographic scope; development capacity; marketing capacity; funding capacity.

- *History*: management experience; culture; portfolio; growth; ambition; product differentiation.

- *Ownership*: public; private; venture-capital funded; family.

In the selection of a menu for a meal, the choice of courses will each have a bearing upon the other and moreover on the choice of wine. So if the company is family owned and funded, and has a management with narrow experience as well as a low history of growth, we see that there is already a pattern which suggests that highly innovative biological products with a need for extensive investment in manufacturing and broad scale clinical development will not be attractive to that company. In big pharma, however, while anything could be considered, the preference is unlikely to be for niche products with only local market opportunities.

The internal review therefore sets out the ballpark in which the most likely candidate attributes can be broadly defined. Once again while there should be no absolute barrier to innovation it will nevertheless be tempered by the broader constraints. The thing that needs to be derived is a 'perfect product profile' to suit each of the needs of the company. Although the chances of matching this ideal in the market are extremely small, without a clear idea of the actual need, an evaluation of the multitude of available products becomes much harder. The more the profile of the product can be made objective in its view, the more exacting the analysis of the search results becomes. I have called this view of the perfect profile an 'opportunity anatomy' as it serves to describe all the attributes of the desired products from an internal and external perspective and describes the relationship between the factors which will make the opportunity work in the context of the company, together with its portfolio and the marketplace in which it operates. The method is not complex but the degree of sophistication brought to the thinking in the model which it creates will be highly instructive at the later stages of a transaction, as it can set the level of desire and therefore gives some idea of the value of a product which matches the perfect profile. By distinction it assists in the valuation of the products which come close but are not perfect. Another useful feature is that it also helps management decision-making through an assessment of their tolerance for deviations from the ideal.

Internal landscape	Market	Product Attributes	Weighting
Size	Size	IP	+ to +++++
Geography	Growth	Preclinical package	
Development capacity	Segmentation	History	
Marketing	Competition	Stage	
Funding	Development level	Difficulty	
Management experience	Promotional responsiveness	Portfolio fit in development	
Customers	Prescriber focus	Portfolio fit in the market	
Growth	Patient turnover	Results	
Ambition	Seasonality	Regulatory pathway	
Product differentiation		Manufacturing	
Ownership private/public		Cost of goods	

Figure 3.9   Opportunity attributes

Internal landscape

SIZE

Each company size will be relative to the opportunity and must be taken in the context of the other attributes yet when considered in isolation a small company can only have limited ambitions in pharmaceutical terms. A blockbuster launch is beyond the ability of a small company unless they have a large partner. Medium-sized companies probably have the greatest potential for growth in that they have enough resources and the ability to raise funds for quite sizeable product developments with the capacity to convert much of the opportunity into revenues for themselves without having to share with a partner or partners.

Large companies have a different burden, because generating growth from a large base is much more difficult. Products in this context cannot become attractive until they are able to generate sums in the hundreds of millions or greater per year in sales. Below a critical size in each company the use of resources needed to develop a small product becomes uneconomic, as the returns cannot match those used to develop a successful large product. Consequently the partial development of a product which then fails to fulfil its potential for some reason, such as label restrictions, becomes an opportunity for smaller companies with a different economic scale and, as a result, the product becomes the object of out-licensing.

GEOGRAPHY

Being a local player in pharmaceuticals markets can carry either a penalty or an advantage. Larger products are most often licensed to companies who can provide extensive reach, worldwide by preference. The licensor has a much lower management risk through having fewer licensees and will benefits from a continuity of support. Conversely a local player may have preferential access to particular markets in a particular geography which will improve its profile as a partner.

DEVELOPMENT CAPACITY

Assuming that the company has an internal development capacity as several companies outsource this function, there will be a preference for those areas where staff have experience and expertise. Clinical development is a costly exercise and most companies will do well to extend their range only gradually, building on their core competencies. Even where a development team can be acquired with a product, know-how and insight are not easily handed on during the technology transfer period. Alongside the experience there may also be the physical capacity issues – say, if activities must be carried on offsite, problems in oversight and management can occur and so jeopardize the development programme. The standards of documentation, operating procedures and compatibility with the regulatory function within a company will all have a bearing on the attractiveness of an opportunity.

MARKETING CAPACITY

The ability of an organization to acquire and develop a product does not automatically imply that when it is brought to market it will be necessarily be a success. The company's capacity to commercialize the product needs to start well before launch and will involve teams in the design of the clinical support studies leading up to the launch and beyond, including the introduction of the product to opinion leaders and through them to centres of excellence. These activities need to be continued with labelling support studies to elaborate and substantiate the claims that can be made for the product. It is from these that the product positioning statements can be evolved for the marketing campaign and the materials to support the sales teams across the various countries, cultures and languages where the products will be marketed. The marketing capacity therefore needs to encompass the regulatory negotiators, the medical marketing function, the brand management team and the country-specific product managers and sales directors. Also of importance is the logistics management in the supply chain to ensure that the product is produced, packaged and delivered to across the globe with properly prepared package inserts and that SPCs (Specification of Product Characteristics), quality analysis releases and the reimbursement approvals are in place. Also required will be the product identification procedures, pharmacovigilance programmes and safety reporting database communications.

FUNDING CAPACITY

Depending on the situation of the company the ability to fund a transaction may come from one or more sources. Young companies might seek funding from private sources, from banks, government loans, or venture capital. Only rarely will small companies have significant reserves or income with which to fund development activities of acquired companies. In the middle range of companies where there is some history of trading it may be that there are some retained earnings which may be used for business development. It is often the case in family-owned companies that growth will be funded from retained profits. In publicly traded companies the retention of too much cash in the business can expose a company to the risk of takeover hence it is quite common to see such reserves being used to secure leverage or other debt instruments to fund business development. Large companies will have the option to fund business development directly from revenue, from reserves or, depending on the lending rates at the time, they may use these resources as collateral to secure debt either in the form of short-term instruments or perhaps long-term ones, such as through bond issues either secured against this collateral or convertible into shares in the company when the value of the business development activity has been realized and the share price has risen and can then compensate the bondholders.

Naturally the most efficient method will be employed to achieve the desired result, and it is the capacity of the company to service the funding mechanism which will determine the cost of this capital. The lower their capacity the higher the risk and cost will be to secure the funding. The risk in the product must therefore have a full compensating value to justify the investment. Although the pharmaceuticals industry is high risk, it becomes possible to find funds in most cases due to the high rewards available for success.

The overall funding requirement therefore needs to take into account the cost of the acquisition, the development costs, the marketing costs and the cost of capital. Only if the whole equation works and yields a positive result which includes all these elements will management be able to make a judgement on the suitability of the investment for the company. In structuring transactions therefore it is extremely common to see the initial exposure, the upfront costs, a licence or an acquisition deferred as much as possible to reduce the risk in the transaction for the acquiring company and its shareholders. Funding capacity thus often becomes one of the main constraints of deal selection in business development.

MANAGEMENT EXPERIENCE

Generally managements are hired and paid according to their experience. It is their insight, born of making and surviving mistakes, which informs their next decision. This can of course lead to problems for if a management has succeeded in the past only through a cautious approach, or equally, if nothing has ever gone seriously wrong, the capacity of the management to make bold enough decisions may be impaired as adversity is a great teacher and stimulator of innovation. As the saying goes 'necessity is the mother of all invention'. Even so each management style will have its strengths. Because business development is required to be innovative and so a little iconoclastic in its approach, in dealing with a cautious management it is usually best to remember another old saying: 'The boss may not always be right but he's always the boss.' As a result business development has to understand the experience base of the management in the company and so its preferences when seeking opportunities. This understanding should also be extended to adopting the style and even the 'spin' when proposing them. Management's experience can sometimes be somewhat narrow leading to difficulties in communicating the potential of an opportunity. It is frequently the case that business development has the problem of finding good opportunities and presenting them only to have the opportunity rejected because the management 'couldn't see it', which is frustrating and wasteful. Among my own experiences some proposals succeeded and some did not; those opportunities were lost purely because my audience didn't get the point I was trying to make. The reasons for this were most often that the chance to present the opportunity came at the wrong moment. CEOs are typically extremely busy so, since you may be thrust into the limelight in an elevator or on a flight, the ability to 'pitch' your project rapidly and well can be a useful skill. Included in the opportunity anatomy therefore is the need to understand the psychology and mentality of the company's management and where the 'hot buttons' are; meaning that the business development group must be intimate with management on a daily basis to keep abreast of any changes in mood or priority. Knowing this can avoid much wasted effort in pursuing propositions which will not be attractive later.

CUSTOMER PORTFOLIO

When seeking the criteria for a transaction business development also needs to be mindful of the customer base of the company. Unless the company is extremely diversified some areas will always be a poor fit. Certain specialty areas are clearly not for the generalist; for example women's health, in vitro fertilization and contraception are served by specialists in medicine who require specialist knowledge and support from of their product suppliers. In the medical device markets, surgical devices for use in internal medicine do not sit comfortably with the osteology products such a spinal implants. Dermatology, gastrointestinal medicine, cardiology, neurology, to name some of the areas of hospital medicine which have highly technical requirements, require an equivalent specialization from the personnel in the company to match their needs. The intricacies of each sector demand a focused group with complementary skills in product development and understanding of market dynamics like patient management, reimbursement and specialist diagnostic requirements. By contrast primary care requires a breadth of knowledge which can address the needs of a practitioner who must make a preliminary diagnosis and initial treatment or the decision to make a referral for specialist intervention. This needs a different approach and, in selling medicines, through the provision of sufficient evidence to support initial use of a product.

Alongside these are specialty areas such as the provision of vaccines at local level or negotiating for government contracts (a market with opportunities and constraints which are very different to either those of the hospital or those of primary care therapeutic markets). Hence the compatibility of an opportunity with the business of the company, defined as its customers, is an issue of crucial importance in setting up the parameters for a desirable product.

GROWTH

There are a number of aspects to growth which must be considered in the backdrop to a product profile. If your company is in a rapid growth phase, the addition of a management intensive product will be more of a challenge than that of a more 'standard' product. Conversely if the company's growth is stagnant the injection of a rapidly growing product or dynamic development opportunity can invigorate the whole company. There are major considerations surrounding growth which are affected by the management and financial aspects discussed above. There may also be the development capacity constraints that might follow the acquisition of a major programme, especially if this were a smaller company. Runaway growth can be dangerous to any company and is often referred to as 'over-trading' in the sense that the company cannot service the market opportunity either physically, in that it cannot produce enough stock, or financially, when it cannot fund either manufacturing or development from its revenues. On the other hand, starving an existing business to fund a new opportunity also has its downsides. As a result it is wise to consider the impact of a product in the context of the company's existing growth and what effect there might be from the product's growth and its requirement for resources as a consequence. These elements will help to profile likely candidates in the evolution of this process.

AMBITION

The ambition of the management and investors, where this is different, has also to be taken into consideration which will be borne out of the history of the company, the expectations of the shareholders and investors and the personality of the individuals involved. Where there is significant bias toward science and medicine the ambition of the company is often driven towards growth in order to fund the research and development needs of the products. This can be a powerful motivator. Where, however, an individual and their team are motivated more towards using the company to generate value, measured in financial terms or perhaps as the means to express personal power through capital, then a different ethos will take hold. It is true to say that this only refers to the dominant motive; the majority of business people in pharmaceuticals are very much concerned with the delivery of higher-quality medicines and the advancement of science and accept that to achieve this they must make use of considerable capital resources. There has, however, been a recent trend towards growth through acquisition and the development of the specialty pharmaceutical sector has shown that a more business-like approach can be a successful means to both the creation of new medicines and a spectacular generator of shareholder value and personal wealth. Excellent examples of success in generating this kind of growth are Shire Pharmaceuticals and Reliant Pharmaceuticals. In creating the business development response to a management's ambition it is therefore important to bring the dimension of ambition into play as it will have a significant bearing on the valuation process and approaches to negotiation. The business-dominated approach may be more likely to look at an asset for its tradeable value in the medium term rather than its long-term medicinal value, particularly if the company has been funded by venture capital or a buy-out fund. Hence in these situations a more adventurous proposal may be well received. More cautious managements frequently require that a greater depth of analysis and due diligence be conducted before considering and committing to a transaction. This is not to say that both approaches do not have their merits and successes, but for business development the mindset of the management will remain a major influencing factor.

PRODUCT DIFFERENTIATION

Product differentiation can at times mean the opportunity to diversify risk in a company or alternatively may be a strategic foray into new and uncharted territory where competition is low or absent. For many organizations 'sticking to their knitting', as the saying goes, is an important expression of focus and effective utilization of resources. The balance to be struck between these two views depends on the interplay between many of the other factors mentioned previously and must be judged according to the ambient circumstances and the future position the company wishes to achieve. The strategic and tactical differences between the existing portfolio and the new products will need to remain consistent with the need to grow and the capacity of the current markets to provide the opportunity for that growth. If the company is in a big market but severely hampered by competition it may be extremely useful for it to enter some smaller and less competitive niche markets to bolster growth. Alternatively if steady exploitation of an expanding market share is providing good growth, the wise and fruitful course may well be through developing the franchise through line extensions and complementary products. Evaluation of the impact of a business development opportunity on the overall shape of the portfolio is required to ensure harmony and best use of assets to achieve results.

OWNERSHIP

Whether the company has public or private status can have a significant bearing on the evaluation of the business development opportunity. When value, price, economic impact, portfolio fit and strategic intent of the company are on public show and analysts from many different investors are making their own assessments of the wisdom, or otherwise, of a transaction many more questions must be addressed and answered than in privately held companies. This is especially true if the majority shareholders are also active in the board of the company. The argumentation offered by business development on behalf of a project to management in a public company must satisfy a full corporate decision-making and governance process; an individual owner, with no one else to answer to, can be as idiosyncratic as they please up to a point. Although this seems a simplistic view there have been a good many European companies where until recently individuals or family groups still controlled the final decision. This model has since reduced in significance since several families have sold their stakes in their companies as the industry consolidates.

Venture-backed companies form a distinct group within privately held companies, with different agendas. Here individuals representing venture firms hold board seats and can bring considerable influence to bear on a board's decisions about business development issues. They are principally concerned, however, with their own portfolios and sometimes this takes priority for them over the interests of the company, with negative results. Over the last decade in both investing and consulting I have observed decisions taken to in-license or out-license products based not, as it should be, on the best outcome for the company but on the willingness or ability of a venture fund to provide more money for the transaction. If the transaction requires additional funding commitments which would overly concentrate the venture fund's portfolio of investments in one company or if it would result in the need to bring in further investors, and would thus dilute the venture fund's share of the equity in the company, reducing their influence on the board and control of the investment, the fund may veto it. The status of the company's shareholding will thus have a major structural impact on any transaction because of the downstream effects of financing the operations of the product afterwards.

This last part in the evaluation of the internal landscape demands that each business development transaction must be approached in the context of all these influences for the given situation. The transaction must be chosen to suit the internal and external landscapes and be presented to appeal to the influencers and decision-makers and deliver value in a way which enhances the company's future across all these dimensions.

External landscape

When selecting the market or markets to search for opportunities, several determinants of the choice will thus be prescribed by the internal constraints. The features which will be under this influence include the size and growth of the market. A vast market may superficially look like a great opportunity, yet if its growth is stagnant it will pose a major promotional challenge. A rapidly growing market may equally look attractive on the outside but might be the subject of rapid technical evolution, with short product life cycles and quick substitution; it would therefore offer a cash flow of only limited duration and a company would need to recoup development costs very rapidly in order to show a profit. This latter market type is often seen in medical devices and diagnostic products where technical innovation can speed ahead and is often combined with shorter regulatory approval times than pharmaceuticals so reducing barriers to market entry and encouraging fierce competition. New product adoption can thus change the market much more rapidly than would normally be the case in pharmaceutical markets. Indeed the need for rapid deal evaluation is increasing throughout the health care industry as competition for product opportunities hots up. Gone are the days when a big pharmaceutical company could take 9 months or a year to evaluate a licensing opportunity; the need now is to evaluate at speed, which requires appropriate tools to discriminate between opportunities. An interesting example of extreme product life cycle compression is the snack sector, where new product developments may only be given a maximum of 6 weeks to succeed or be withdrawn. Innovative products are tested in small areas and a managed through in-store promotions and local advertising to see if the product has consumer potential or not during that short period of time. Intensive market research is carried out to establish if the product has consumer potential but the ultimate determinant is off-shelf movement. If this does not develop the product is dropped. While such development and marketing cycles are unheard of in biotech and pharmaceutical markets because of the technical and regulatory hurdles involved, the thinking which goes into the pursuit of a business transaction in health-care needs to incorporate some of the same characteristics in order to be effective and competitive. The long drawn out testing of samples in the laboratory or in animal models slows the business development process as too few projects can be evaluated. As more data are generated, decision-making can become blurred if the discriminating characteristics identified as satisfying the market in the first place are not adhered to.

Apart from questions of size and growth, the ability to segment a market to assist market penetration may be a positive aspect. However, if there is fragmentation not segmentation this could become a barrier to market share growth ('fragmentation' describes small unconnected and uneconomic groups and 'segmentation' seeks to create groupings which are large enough to merit investments in product development and marketing). However, some diseases are intrinsically too small to be economically attractive for drug development. This has led to the provision of special support for small patient groups in so-called 'orphan indications' where the numbers of patients are few yet the cost of product development remains high. Except where such support exists there is little incentive to invest which is why a segmentation exercise is so valuable in evaluating a product opportunity.

COMPETITION

The competitors in a market must also be stringently assessed for their size, strength, reputation, aggression and number. A market may have a single dominant player or it may be shared among many players of different sizes. The competitive nature of the market is a good indicator of the cost of entry and the cost of maintaining market share, and these costs will have an impact on the market's attraction. The history of competition in a market is often overlooked in this assessment and its effect on the evolution of the market should be noted. Due account should also be taken of technical innovations. A number of additional factors need to be considered as aspects of competition: chief amongst which are patient turnover and responsiveness to promotion.

Patient turnover

Patient turnover is critical to effective competition. An excellent case in point was the angina market in the UK in the 1980s. Many new products were being launched and were expanding the market's value considerably. The older glyceryltrinitrate products and other coronary vasodilators were giving way to new long-acting forms such as the isosorbide dinitrate and mononitrate and these were being augmented by the introduction of newer coronary vasodilators such as calcium channel blockers. At that time my task was to introduce one of these calcium channel blockers to the market. The launch, which was late due to regulatory delays, firstly had to contend with the dominant competitor, nifedipine, and secondly a cheaper and often generically available group of products based on verapamil. After the early stages of the launch were over my team were perplexed to find that, despite a good reception and enthusiasm amongst doctors in the key prescribing group for our product, sales were sluggish. After some market research and analysis it became clear that it was not the selling and promotion of this or the size of the market that was holding back growth: it was the rate at which the patients had their prescriptions reviewed and changed. We were promoting the product well in hospitals and in primary care but were achieving steady but only linear growth. The prescribing pattern showed that patients would be reviewed by their physicians every 3 months and, of these a certain percentage would be changed to a new product. This would not be done in primary care: the patient would be sent to the local hospital to be evaluated and switched to a new product. The market research revealed that each hospital doctor was changing 1.84 patients per month on average and when multiplied by the total number of doctors in hospitals this exactly matched the rate of our new prescriptions. In order to penetrate the market faster we had to accelerate the rate of patient turnover, which is what we did: we promoted the need for primary care practices to call in patients with a poor history of success or compliance and refer them on to the hospitals. The competition in this case was less other companies' promotion than the structural resistance of the market to change.

Responsiveness to promotion

This is the other aspect of competition. It is illustrated in part by the previous example. It is also heavily affected by the technical complexity of the product. Simple products for trivial illnesses are changed frequently by the doctor when they are given high enough levels of effective promotion as the consequences of a change are not likely to be significant. Technical products do not respond to promotional weight alone, however. Technical products require a much greater body of evidence to satisfy the burden of proof a doctor will demand before they adopt a product, because an ill-informed choice of a drug used in for instance the treatment of heart disease could be fatal. The approach required in promoting technical products needs to be one that respects the particular requirements of that specific market and tailors the provision of information to the audience. Each physician will need to see that comprehensive testing and evaluation by reputable colleagues has been performed before placing sufficient trust in a product to risk relying on its effectiveness on behalf of a patient. In highly technical markets there tends to be a concentration of prescribing doctors who are specialists in particular areas. The more exotic the disease the more likely it is that only a few physicians will have gained the knowledge and the experience to treat patients successfully. From the business development perspective this can offer a market with a much reduced cost of promotion and so may be accessible to smaller, and sometimes newer, companies. Depending on the value of the disease to the patient and their families this is this can also mean that the rewards of supplying smaller sectors can be high. One only has to think of in-vitro fertilization, and treatments for single-gene or enzyme-dependent disorders such as cystic fibrosis, Fabry's and Gaucher's diseases, to see examples of small patient numbers generating considerable value to companies of moderate size.

Another factor to be considered in selecting a market as a suitable target for promotion is its stage of development, as the competitive aspects will vary considerably between stages. Markets can be in several different states beyond big and small, growing or declining. The new market with few products and a lower level of functional satisfaction can be wide open to novel technical solutions. Bigger markets naturally require the more educational and promotional cost yet the classic example of H_2 antagonists leading on to the adoption of proton pump inhibitors is economic incentive enough to justify these expenses. This was described in part above in the example of Zantac, the H_2 blocker, and Prilosec, the proton pump inhibitor, as they fought for dominance of the prescription market in the USA. The market evolved from antacids to Tagamet, the first of the H_2 blockers; this was supplanted by Prilosec and subsequent proton pump inhibitors, and its successful conversion to non-prescription status has generated and maintains a multi-billion-dollar treatment franchise. The inadequacy of antacids in the face of peptic and duodenal ulceration and gastrointestinal (GI) inflammation was clear in the marketplace and the reduction in the incidence of ulceration and GI inflammation is a testament to the effectiveness of the new agents which have been adopted first as prescription products and then as over the counter (OTC) products by doctors and patients alike. Yet 'price efficient' markets where there has been no technical innovation and so where generic price levels abound have deterred innovation for many years in a number of cases. The cystitis and urinary incontinence markets are just two examples where patients have not benefited from any truly major technical advances for many years. Product introductions into markets of this kind have very different characteristics to novel product introductions into 'technical' or 'trivial' markets. When a technically superior product to treat foot infections, which could justify a premium price, was released, the dormant market for systemic antifungals responded to this innovation, research into the area was revived and competition was stimulated.

A final major influence which must be considered in market selection is seasonality. Especially in a portfolio context this can either be the perfect justification for a product or the opposite. Seasonal products are highly demanding of resources at particular times of the year and this places heavy demands on production, on sales and on supply chain support, one after the other. In a normal portfolio to have one such product can be highly disruptive because of the variable effects on inventory holdings, selling time and cash flow requirements. In an ideal situation a company would have a matched 'pair' of cyclical portfolio products (winter/summer) to counterbalance each other with the production and sales seasons neatly dovetailed one into the other. Sadly this is not easily achieved but in product acquisitions seasonal considerations should be thought about in relation to infections, allergies, vaccines and seasonal migrations at holiday times.

Intellectual property

The most frequently considered product attributes are technical or qualitative in nature; however, there are also issues such as Intellectual Property Rights (IPR – or more often just IP) where its quantity must also be matched or exceeded by its quality. A patent must not only be in existence, it must be written in such a form as to be enforceable and defensible. Fundamentally the IP of a company is actually the asset of principle value as it protects the premium for the patent holder or the licensee over other providers. The depth and breadth of the individual patents and the patent estate confer the duration and durability of the cash flows that the products can generate. Yet if the language used to frame the claims is too loose or too tight, or the claims made are too broadly defined, the value can be diluted by challenges and even by being overturned. All it takes for a patent to be invalidated is the existence of prior art or the failure to adequately demonstrate an inventive step – this can undermine or negate years of work and investment. So if the definition of the product is to be attractive for a business development transaction the strength and length of the patent is crucial for success.

PRE-CLINICAL

Alongside the IP claims the preclinical package of a product is a major asset or drawback depending on the quality of the work done and the documentation surrounding it. Solid laboratory work and laboratory notes are required to underpin later submissions and the package needs to address all issues that have been raised as concerns about the compound family before, as well as establishing novel features about the product which will set it apart from competitors at later stages of development. The biological and chemical data are fundamental to the formulation and development of a compound into a medicine of value to patients and companies. The evaluation also has to address the history of a compound depending on the stage of development. Questions of whether a proof of concept has been established in animal models and then validated in man will be enhanced by a clear understanding of the mode of action of the drug from an established scientific model.

PORTFOLIO CONSIDERATIONS

In establishing the desired stage of development for compounds the portfolio needs to be clearly understood as there is often a desire to have a balanced portfolio from the point of view of clinical phase. But what does a balanced portfolio look like?

The differences between a product for pain and a product for arthritis is measured in years and millions invested. If a company has many projects at an early stage of development it is clear that there will be a long time before these will generate income. However, a 'late stage' compound in phase IIb, where safety is being assessed, may still have several years of expensive clinical trials to complete before filing for registration and approval can be made. In cardiovascular trials, in particular heart failure and other chronic conditions, a large number of patients are required to demonstrate effectiveness and the duration of each patient's therapy plus the time for the required follow-up examinations and the analysis of data all take many years. In considering the kind of products to be sought one must consider the cost burden, financing and scientific risks in the plan. The criteria set by and for business development in searching for appropriate candidates need therefore to have a strong rationale.

If the criteria are well understood before discussions with another company are embarked upon, this can save a deal of time and effort. From a personal point of view there is nothing more annoying than to be engaged in a process with a prospective partner who does not have a clear understanding of their own needs. They don't know when to say yes and don't know when to say no. As a result discussions can drag on for months with no way of resolving the engagement until either one side or the other makes an executive decision to summarily halt discussions. It is better to know that a product or project will fail the screen early and move on to a better project.

The development stage and its implications are one aspect of product selection. Another is the marketing environment required to capitalize on the investment in development. There are a number of dimensions to this, including the current marketed portfolio and the company's reliance on this income for operating profits both at the time of launch and beyond. The current therapeutic focus of the company before launching into a new area will be more or less compatible with the requirements of the new product. It will determine the need for any internal reorganization or addition of resources and training to become prepared for the launch. Moreover the sheer cost of a competitive launch may require considerable additional finance which may bring resource constraints to other parts of the company. Although there are ways of optimizing each of these factors, such as leveraging more finance or partnering through co-promotion, there are many different ways of resolving a less than ideal situation which by negotiation may be decisive in the choice to pursue one business development opportunity over another. Even so it is a brave management that will choose to finance a radical change in portfolio direction without strong reserves or no viable alternatives. Depending on the scale of such a reorganization or refinancing, a number of alternatives may have to be considered to balance company resources and accommodate such a launch. These might include borrowing significant funds in the short term until the launch costs have been recouped or setting up a co-promotion partnership to share the costs, but with the proviso that the profits must also be shared. The choice of one business development opportunity over another will thus need to take the funding and resource requirements into consideration and where major structural changes would be required to achieve success this could tip the balance in favour of one opportunity over another, depending on the views of the management and of the investors. Although a radical change in the business model, perhaps through an acquisition, might be attractive from one point of view it would be unusual for investors to take such a risk without the prospect of considerable rewards.

One of the critical features of a product is its differentiation from others in the market. It has long been my belief that successful products have to have some truly differentiating feature if they are to have a good chance in the market. There is an inherent problem in the market in that the costs and uncertainties of drug development can lead to a number of similar products being developed simultaneously and, if they all succeed, the result will be many poorly differentiated products coming to market not because they are needed but because, if the development has not failed, the costs must be recouped to whatever degree is possible. The process of choosing a product which will have a differentiated profile will be dealt with later but, no matter how it is achieved, it is a crucial element.

When addressing this issue the differentiation should be of a functional rather than a theoretical nature. By this I mean that achieving a clinical result merely by a more sophisticated means actually has little value. Much has been written for instance about the differentiation between celecoxib (a COX_2 inhibitor) versus naproxen. Both products' protagonists have put forward arguments to support the theoretical advantages of each product in its effects on stomach and heart issues. However, only if the practical benefits can be seen by patients and physicians will they translate into market share notwithstanding any weight of promotional expenditure. I was involved with the area of ulcer treatments in the UK in the lead-up to the launch of omeprazole in the 1980s and saw that no matter what else the Glaxo team tried as a defence for ranitidine, the speed of onset of symptomatic relief of omeprazole could not be denied. Surely and steadily the market moved to proton-pump inhibitors such as omeprazole, not for theoretical reasons but because its effect was tangibly faster and so better for the patient.

An issue which may seem an obvious qualification for selection for portfolio is the clinical results that the product has demonstrated to date in its development. Despite even dramatic clinical evidence in anecdotal studies it is sometimes difficult to establish the worth of a product without strong comparative clinical evidence and this has to be established in a manner which will be accepted by the regulatory authorities and furthermore can be replicated in a real-world clinical setting. Poorly controlled studies including poorly performed statistical analysis or confounding factors can negate even a very promising drug candidate's attractions. The potential of social factors influencing the drug's acceptability to patients, of unforeseen drug interactions, of selective analysis, of data omissions or of recruitment errors in clinical studies have all cropped up as reasons in due diligence for rejecting products for in-licensing and investment.

In combination with the need to demonstrate differentiation, providing substantial proof is paramount. A clear example of such a breakdown in development occurred after we had taken a product through to very late-stage licensing discussions. The product was a chemical castrator, and it had a sound mode of action and encouraging preclinical and clinical results. The differentiating feature of this product was claimed to be a complete lack of 'hot flashes' suffered by patients through suppression of testosterone production: this was the drawback of the multi-billion dollar market leader. Yet despite the drug's mode of action theoretically not permitting the 'hot flashes' to occur, as the studies progressed unexplained 'flash' occurrences happened to patients on the active substance. With the first hot flash report, our product profile was destroyed. All we had was a similar drug to the market leader with a lower frequency of adverse events – not a real functional advantage, certainly not enough to support the premium price which would be required to pay for the development and marketing costs.

As already suggested by the issues raised about the regulatory pathway, the pathway itself needs to be clearly defined. In investing in early-stage products it is not always easy to see the hurdles that will be placed in front of the products by regulatory agencies and their advisors. It is, however, possible to see what has been done before and estimate the likely impact of unanswered questions on the time to approval for a product. Clearly the most difficult path is the one which has not been trodden before. On more than one occasion I've been involved with projects where the regulators themselves have not had a precedent for an approval path. In one of these cases the product had been proposed as a means to avoid complications of surgery called 'post-operative adhesions'. However, there are still no reasonable statistics available on the incidence of these complications. Despite many specialists and surgeons acknowledging the seriousness of these adhesions the root cause they gave in interviews was these were always a result of 'poor technique' and of course the specialists 'never saw' this in their own practice. As a result the company had to propose a means to measure the success of their products against a 'ghost' problem. The study design they were forced to adopt required follow-up surgery to confirm the incidence of the complication. The number of volunteers to undergo a second procedure was, not surprisingly, very low and the study timeline extended way beyond the original estimates. The eventual approval of the product in the US came 5 years after the study was proposed and that despite the product being on the market in the EU all that time. Needless to say, the economics of the products were unrecognizable when compared to the original plan.

Another raft of issues which must be reflected in the screening process exists in the manufacturing base. These may be technical or environmental in nature or could be caused by constraints on resources. If there is insufficient internal capacity it may be necessary to outsource the manufacture of some or all of the required components. Few companies now manufacture their own active product ingredient (API) and many will incorporate delivery devices sourced and invented externally. Outsourcing has become one of the keys to profit in manufacturing. But with outsourcing comes the need for extensive due diligence in deal-making as the manufacturing standards, contracts and financial security of every component manufacturer must be attended to during the deal-making process. As well as the regulatory qualification of the manufacturing site, the need for visits by FDA and EMEA inspectors can occasionally prove to be problematic. This was the case for a client whose manufacturing site was in Israel during one of the recent crises. The FDA inspectors were embargoed by the Agency from visiting a designated war zone. Without inspection the site could not be approved and, lacking approval, all the test batches required for the marketing authorization could not be submitted. This put pressure on the company as they could neither launch the product nor use the batches, which were perishable and so went out of date waiting for inspection.

Manufacturing has very well-defined project planning and the vagaries of politics and regulations can severely affect the timelines and cost. So if the final synthetic pathway is not established or the API sourcing comes from distant lands it may be better to choose another opportunity.

The final item in the screening test is the cost of goods (CoGs). Naturally everything we have previously discussed will have a marked effect on the CoGs but as an independent variable it is a pivotal issue in deciding for or against a product. Optimization of synthesis can reduce the CoGs to some extent but this needs to be balanced against the capital cost of any new plant required for a new synthesis, or the introduction of new machinery for formulation work or even packaging. Furthermore all of these will require regulatory approval at each step of the way and be subject to the approval process timelines which typically are 60- or 90-day review times even if there are no questions.

Another example of the vagaries of manufacturing occurred when reviewing the cost of goods of a new formulation of capsules during the final review it came to light for the first time that the machines required to complete the filling would not fit the building on the chosen manufacturing site. The machines were too tall for the ground floor and too heavy for the upper floors and so required a new facility to be built solely for this product which reduced the operating margin by several per cent until the costs could be written down.

Exotic methods of production with untried and so not previously approved pathways have many issues depending on the risk tolerance of the company, its investors or the management proposing such a product can have a far-reaching effect on the fate of the company. Search criteria therefore need to be tailored to the current and future situation of the company and rigorously applied in screening opportunities. There are very few right choices but very many wrong ones and, at the risk of seeming too exacting, and so passing up what looks like a good product, experience has shown that by being hard-headed about these criteria at the earliest opportunity many a bullet can be dodged.

Profiling and Searching for Opportunities

One of the most frequent questions I hear is: 'Where do you find your opportunities?' Truthfully the answer to this question can be less systematically applied than can that to many others. The increasing sophistication of the licensing and business development communities across the globe are still not a total solution for any or all companies. The existence of licensing and partnering conferences, websites and journals, together with specialized agencies acting as clearing houses and the technology transfer offices of the major universities and hospitals, have increased the number of opportunities available; but in some ways this proliferation clouds the view rather than helping. There is no standard method of presentation or equality of knowledge about where, when and how to make an opportunity available, or indeed any common purpose in seeking a partner. The range of opportunities is extremely broad, varying from product ideas to marketed products and from novel drug targets to complex devices and technologies to enhance the practice of medicine. Patents may range from covering a surgical procedure to the invention of a new chemical compound, and on to a gene, to the design of a device or, the software that runs it. All of these can be found if you know where to look and what your need may be: a strategy is needed to reduce wasted effort and to find suitable candidates.

There are two basic landscapes to investigate when conducting a search, the first is the internal – who and what do we know already? – and the second is external. The former is quite often overlooked in the search process by business development departments and most frequently comes to light when an internal review team is asked to assess an opportunity and someone says, 'Oh but I did this 5 years ago' or, 'You should've talked to 'X' about it – she's been working on this for years.' As long as the criteria have been properly selected and are clear it can be relatively easy to investigate internal sources of knowledge in research and development and to follow up their contacts. The more often this is tried the more familiar the company's R&D organization will become with thinking proactively about new opportunities and, incidentally, it may also become more objective about rejection of a project. Internal R&D personnel sources are apt to judge opportunities primarily on their scientific attractions so it is a good idea to explain the business criteria before asking for suggestions to avoid the creation of a champion for a lost cause and with it the problems this brings. From experience, however, brainstorming sessions with senior scientists looking for ideas on whom to contact makes good use of their in-depth knowledge of where the best research is being conducted and which groups have innovative ideas. A frequent and open dialogue between business development and the research function makes good use of this major resource and if handled tactfully encourages scientists to participate in the creative side of the business in an informative way. However, there is always the potential for this to take on the appearance of a committee in charge of decisions if carried too far: the process must remain in the hands of business development to maintain portfolio continuity. Informality should, I suggest, be a key element of such interactions.

Scientists are not the only internal sources of information useful to the business development person. Others who have a significant knowledge of the industry work in patenting, where the competition is constantly monitored for their competitive and potentially infringing activities. Manufacturing is also a good source of competitive intelligence regarding new techniques such as in formulation and delivery devices. Marketing and sales internationally and in affiliate companies will also have a perspective on what is happening in the marketplace in that they can help to validate what the market wants or believes it wants since they are in direct contact with the physicians, technicians and patients.

The increasing specialization of business development brings with it the danger of the function becoming isolated from its peers, and this should be guarded against. If business development seeks a special role in the company it should be by consensus that this is a required function and not an imposition by management. Talk abounds of business development having to 'sell' its ideas hard to overcome the internal resistance: this speaks of a function which has become divorced from the heart of the business. In part this may be a result of where business development reports into the organization. Is it the CEO or the CFO? Sometimes business development or a part of the function becomes a subdivision of R&D which can lead to separate agendas being formed to satisfy inward-facing goals. Close coordination is required to get the best from the portfolio which must be set at corporate level to maintain focus on the overall objective. While the financial function will always come into play in business development there is sometimes a question about the motivation of a business development function managed from the financial base. My view is that the business development role should be generalist and take into account all the drivers on the company's performance. It should be focused on sustainable growth and competitive advantage in the first place rather than being led by one agenda or another.

External sources are more varied and difficult to describe simply because of the diversity described before. This reinforces the need for clarity in identifying the profile of the products or services required to boost growth in the company. The variety of product and project sources prompts some attempt to classify each as the most likely source of a particular kind of opportunity. So, for instance, if a mature product is required the most likely source would be a large pharmaceutical company, not overlooking these as a good source of other assets. Conversely, universities are a great source of novel programmes but they would have no existing products. A loose matrix of opportunities and sources might look like the example in Figure 4.1 and suggest the beginnings of a *search plan*.

Search database

In creating a database for a search the source characteristics and the desired product profile are natural poles on the matrix axes. Other considerations need then to be layered into the search pattern. Two such considerations might be geography or historical activity. These can be good pointers as to where to search, particularly

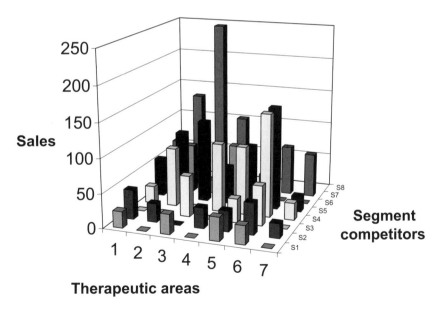

Figure 4.1   Search plan by segment

when allied to such criteria as strength of intellectual property protection in the region or as indicated by publication density of, say, a university in a special area of research. However, the steady march of globalization is progressively breaking down these barriers and business development executives are now travelling well beyond the traditional EU, US and Japanese markets in search of new academic and commercial developments. Korea, Latin America, India, China, Russia and many other areas are making great strides at all levels of research and development through to marketed products and need access to world markets through established distribution channels. Also the WTO and TRIPS initiatives are beginning to ensure greater attention to the need for high-quality clinical work and solid intellectual property (IP) protection. Consequently a search must now include a much wider vision of the geographical possibilities than before, particularly as developments in biological therapies are being achieved without the same degree of reliance on a chemical industry infrastructure for rapid developments which previously localized high-quality developments.

Beyond the institutions of universities and the major research-based pharmaceutical companies there are also a very large number of privately funded research institutes which have a strong health-care focus particularly in medical devices and enabling technologies which can complement drug discovery. There are also some individual physicians, chemists or biologists who are inventors of potentially valuable assets; these last are the least frequent sources of products in pharmaceuticals but can be a useful source of technologies and techniques in device inventions and in surgical techniques.

A new force in health-care development has been the establishment of science parks, business parks, 'technopoles' and clusters which have been funded by national, regional or local government agencies to stimulate the local economy. The these are usually centred around one or more universities and seek to commercialize the research of the university while retaining some value in either the IP of the products and now also the equity in a 'spin out' company. Governmental sponsors see these parks as an important tool in developing economic activity and job creation on a local basis, thus serving the needs of their electors and taxpayers. The different agendas of parks' sponsors can sometimes lead to a lack of clarity as to whether the objective of the park is primarily commercial or an extension of academic research. The park management typically have the responsibility to maintain the focus on the commercial side but if the board composition is strongly academic this can be a difficult path to maintain. Nevertheless, these parks offer opportunities to business development groups as a focus of developing IP and by providing central support for out-licensing activities.

The other main players in the establishment of new companies are the investors. Venture capital funds in particular have portfolio interests which will thrive through the creation of financial or commercial partnerships which enhance the value of their shareholdings. As yet there are few central sources of information derived from investors but larger funds and some associations (EVCA, BIO, EFB) are beginning to make some information available in an organized and useful way for business development through the use of websites and through sponsorship of partnering meetings.

A recent addition to the technoparks and investor groups has been professional associations such as the network of Pharma Licensing Groups (PLGs) and commercial sources such as, pharmalicensing.com and intermediary agencies such as Bridgehead, Bionest and others. These agents operate both as clearing houses for opportunities and can act as retained search agents working on contingency success fees to bring a transaction to fruition. Where such an agency has preferred access through personal connections, intermediary relationships can expedite a search through privileged knowledge and introductions.

Search targets

How then to launch a search for a particular target product? In the first stages the process is ideally kept as simple as possible and this should include a level of desk research before engaging in personal contact by email or telephone. Eliminating the obviously wrong candidates from the search is highly desirable early on and these simple methods can assist in that process, but may also dismiss some opportunities erroneously if the classification is unclear or unwieldy. By use of the product profile which has been derived earlier, a list of potential candidates can be built and equally importantly a list of candidates that are not 'qualified' as suitable and the reasons why this is the case. The accumulated data can be recorded in any number of ways from simple card indexes to computer database tools. In the case of a distributed database, depending on the scale of the company, networked databases including R&D and manufacturing and regulatory functions can make their search and resources available to the business development group and can be most effective. For a small company the centralization of information permits rapid searching and facilitates recall of information, while in the large organization it should be an easily searched resource by a number of people. If successfully implemented it can become a valuable and persistent resource but only if it is well maintained by or on behalf of a series of users over the course of a number of years.

Web-based research

The breadth of the search will similarly be tailored to the resources of the company but with the improvement in web-searching engines the opportunity to search on a worldwide basis becomes much more feasible at the level of the individual if a search method is developed.

Knowledge is made up of an association of facts and beliefs, but is coded in language. Web-based searching permits detailed searching starting with only a hazy idea of the object of the search. Firstly the basic facts can be entered into one or more of the main web search engines, as might be the disease, the type of product, the desired effects for example, *kidney cancer, drug, cure.*

When put into Google this particular example returned 13,200,000 results. The addition of *and* to the search refined it to 5,680,000 and already the top search results mentioned approved drugs. This permits the creation of a list of existing products firstly already in the market, and then in research and in development to be created (see Figure 4.2).

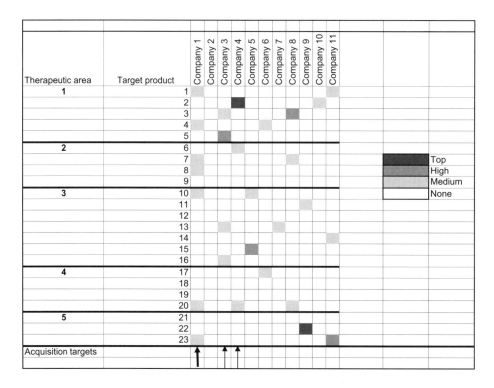

Figure 4.2   Search strategy, by segment, by product, by company

The search strategy can then be progressively refined by narrowing the criteria to address the attributes of the product profile ideally suited to the portfolio in question across several criteria. Inevitably the search will also bring out a great deal of ancillary information, and some of this may actually contradict the assumptions of the profile. For instance if you believe there is little competition among marketed products in the area which interests you, yet you find 20 in development which were previously unknown, this might alter your prioritization of the area. However, the quantity of information retrieved does not speak to the quality of either the information or the truth about the 20 products as web data are often not well maintained particularly if a product's development has already been discontinued. Web pages can be left for several years. You need to ask questions such as: Are they all still in development? At what stage? What is the comparative profile of each to the other? Are the products partnered? Have they been invented by a big company or by a university start-up? All the information you can find must then be classified, weighted and compared across a number of parameters before the active search can begin in earnest. I have characterized this process as 'mapping' the opportunity and from this multidimensional map an 'opportunity anatomy' can be derived (see Figure 4.3). Representing this opportunity anatomy in a two-dimensional matrix may seem useful but has limitations in its ability to communicate the inter-relationships between the component parts.

Visualization methods can end up oversimplifying what is a truly complex situation and lead to false conclusions. Happily this means there is no computer program yet foreseen which can substitute for the business development

Needs factors	Target profile	Functional specification	Class comparators	Market size/growth	Benefits
No pregnancy No bleeding Normal cycle	Single tablet within 48 hrs	Orally bio-available No effect on oestrogen levels Rapid clearance	Ru-486 Plan-B	$800m +15%	Extended cover No detectable SEs No worries

Figure 4.3   Opportunity anatomy: emergency contraception

professional in the job of selecting which opportunities to pursue in the context of the company's business plan. The many dimensions that have been identified in the internal landscape are vastly magnified by the complexity of the real world. The task in business development is, however, to perform the 'art of the possible' and so the refinement of the search criteria can mostly be made by the posing of fairly common-sense questions: Is it available? Is it the best? Is it affordable? Will it succeed? These reality check questions permit selection of a limited list of possible candidates and from these identification of the named company or other sources and ideally the contact name and number of the person in the company or institution can be made.

As a result a prioritized list of company contacts can be created for follow-up and a subset of this can become the target list for business development to approach. Thus the process has proceeded from a simple list of keywords to a refined target group prioritized and partly 'qualified'. This list now needs one or other of two actions. The first may be to very rapidly establish availability – by calling the contact at the counterparty company – to see if they would entertain an approach for a transaction concerning their product. This may provoke them into declining immediately – which will limit the target list further – or they may accept conditionally with more or less enthusiasm and commitment. Alternatively it may be better to start with creating a detailed profile of each of the targets in order to work out a potentially attractive approach. This step will be required in every case but if the initial list is long it might be wise to first weed out any poor prospects in order to save time.

Contact management

Once an approach has been decided the next steps are to find the best way of contacting the 'counterparty'. Again the number of potential targets of interest will dictate the chosen means to some extent, and particularly if business development has a portfolio of mandates to deal with simultaneously but limited resources. There may be cases, however, due to budgetary or portfolio demands where it may be necessary to use all channels of communication at the same time. The difficulty that this brings lies in the quantity of information that is generated by the search process. Accurate and adequate record keeping and progress reporting are a major part of this task. In order to prepare for this, a system of documentation needs to be established before the search starts. Whether this is conducted by an individual in business development or by a dedicated team for a large group will be driven by circumstances. The principle steps to achieving this are:

- Assimilation – collecting information and a recording it.

- Accommodation – collating, ordering and relating it.

- Synthesis – drawing together information to build a business case.

- Crystallization – drawing conclusions are reporting the information.

Knowledge management in this context needs to be applied to a suitable level for the circumstances. There are many sophisticated computer packages, among which are 'Act!' and 'Goldworks', which have been developed to both record and manage contacts, and yet others which have been extended to include decision support software with the objective of discriminating between opportunities, such as the 'Vertical*I' packages for business development. In mergers and acquisitions the package form 'Evaluate' provides an updated database describing transactions, company profiles and valuations derived from bank equity analysis. Each has strengths and weaknesses and different requirements of a business development group may need to utilize several approaches which can test the ability of the group to adhere to the constraints of working within such a packaged approach. For smaller companies the business development group's approach should probably be the simplest possible to achieve the objective of the search. There is little point in having an elaborate decision support program if the decisions required are simple, or few in number. Here a combination of spreadsheets, simple relational databases such as MS Access® and contact management software packages will be enough for the majority of cases. A big company may have to deal with multiple sites across the world and so will have to provide an infrastructure to address the need for coordinated informed actions, integrated packages which can operate over an intranet-wide area network or a virtual private network architecture and give real-time communications by Blackberries or PDAs. These units, when fed by 'push' technologies with content selected by programmed search engines and continually sent by email or message to the user, update the users and permit consolidation of the latest information relevant to active searches. These technologies together with video conferencing, a 'blog' approach and other communication tools suggest the means to integrate information and manage knowledge. Such a service will also require an army to manage the package and sufficient training for the business development team in how to use it. Seamless integration of inputs on a global basis from R&D to salesperson, touching all points in between, is something of a holy grail for big companies not least because technology makes possible some of the wilder fantasies of the information scientist and the senior manager. However, there is an ever present danger of the task of information management taking over from the business objective. For many years I was engaged in establishing call reporting systems for pharmaceutical sales forces and can testify to the difficulties of implementing a software-driven approach just to data recording. Frequently when taking the design brief for the system it became obvious that there was a temptation for management to record irrelevant information 'because they could' and this overcame common sense among some of the sales managers. They were possessed with a desire to control rather than guide their teams by insisting on a 'spy in the car' approach and because of this complicated the system. It also made the learning curve and administrative burden on the representatives high enough to depress sales. Avoiding data gridlock is therefore a major consideration in establishing a recording system for business development. The challenge is to recognize the salient factors required to make a clear decision and ignore the rest. Achieving this of course takes experience and a minimalist approach is usually the safest in the first instance. From the point of view of what data to collect a rule of thumb is that typically the finer the granularity of the data the lesser the impact they will have on the main event.

The need for an attention to detail should not therefore get in the way of watching the big picture in a transaction as it evolves. A good approach to maintaining the big picture view is to break down each of the elements that make it up into a laundry list of items that must be attended to at each stage of the transaction. A methodical approach overcomes the monumental amount of detail required to complete a transaction making the task achievable to a high degree of quality even with slim resources.

Returning to the sources of this information and how to find them on the web is an obvious starting point as has been discussed earlier. However as has been highlighted before, a drawback of web-based information is the amount of outdated or redundant data which are mixed with current and useful information. My own preference is to maintain a watch on the news for several different portals on a regular basis. You can use RSS – 'really simple syndication' – if your connection, as most are now, is 'always on' by flagging areas of interest. RSS can bring you latest news across most of the syndicated news agencies with high frequency, hourly or even faster. From a competitive monitoring perspective it can be extremely useful to have news brought to your attention in this way, even if the frequency is faster than you could normally react to, especially if the criteria are set tightly with relevance to your interests. However, one must restrict the search criteria to avoid being swamped. To complement this specific sweep a broad view is also required so that you do not miss the unusual, unexpected or just downright new information in your field. This can come through main news agencies, vertically channelled sources or specialized websites with searchable criteria on an ad hoc basis. CNN, yahoo, FT and WSJ are all overlapping news services that I regularly use to maintain a world view of general news, economic news, business news and the like as global events will affect local occurrences and can also affect transactions. Travel logistics, exchange rates and fuel costs can all have a bearing on a large transaction and so need monitoring. Industry-specific information can be found by drilling down into, for instance, FT.com by subscription and at biz.yahoo.com. The advantage of using these reporting sites as well as the pure news feeds is for the analysis of company news that goes beyond facts and into speculation adding useful perspectives. An excellent resource of information directly generated by companies is Biomedical Newsanalyzer, which can be very revealing. It provides a transaction alert system based on company press releases and is structured into specialized information areas. It is presented as a searchable database of these company press releases which, as it has built up over the years, now gives an insight into the history and sequence of actions in the market. For US-based companies SEC filings on a quarterly and annual basis also provide detailed insight into the activities of a company through the publication of the management discussion sections in the reports as well as records of stock sales and other significant financial events which can indicate the developing internal situation within the company over time. Various other bodies can provide similar reports, including UK Companies House webcheck and equivalent information sources from company registries across Europe. The combination of search engines, new services, news analysis, vertical market monitors and formal or informal reporting resources makes for a flexible yet very powerful aggregate source of information. This can be supplemented by publications from manufacturing, *European Process Review, Genetic Engineering News, The Business Development and Licensing Journal*, and *LES News* as well as IP and legal newsletters from various law firms and tax practices. Equity analysts and placement firms provide data either free or by subscription and supply specialist views of aspects of the market. But this information is second-hand, and written by the company for specific purposes; the only way a business development transaction can take place is by personal knowledge of the counterparty's situation. This must be acquired actively rather than passively.

Active searching can take place by direct individual contact, by telephone, even to the point of cold-calling a company and asking the switchboard for the right contact. It can be through networks of colleagues in agencies, law firms, advisors and consultants who can put you in touch by phone or by email to a useful contact. Another approach to this can be to hire an agency or consultant to make these calls on a 'blinded' basis to provide a level of confidentiality to the search. Direct approaches may sometimes alert competitors to the possible availability of an asset or point out the potential value of an asset to its owner if handled indiscreetly.

Conferences

The last 10 years has also seen a burgeoning industry in mediated partnering conferences. Twenty years ago conferences were usually arranged around particular information themes such as medical conferences like ASCO, ASH and their European equivalents, and networking occurred and took its course between scientists or business people and others interested in these topics. Lately the value of the networking has begun to overshadow the conference topic to the point where partnering and networking events are held with virtually no regard to a conference theme. Halls of partnering booths are provided and significant efforts are made to prearrange meetings between prospectively interested parties. Business development in this situation is in its element. Individuals in bigger companies may have 20 to 30 previously arranged meetings with prospective partners over 3 to 4 days during the conference. Web-based profiles permit a mutual approach to pre-booking of meetings and the schedules are managed efficiently to bring the parties together at the event. Bio-Europe, Bio-partnering Europe, Biovision, Biosquare, BIO, Eurobiotech Forum, Biobusiness, BioEquity and a host of other events are all well attended frequently to the point where a whole community travels the globe meeting in various cities and hotels regularly, and exchanging news and views in and around business development. These meetings combined with multiple banking conferences dedicated to health-care companies for either public or private equity investors to understand the companies' business cases provide yet another means for companies to network, this time through their banking contacts.

Apart from providing the chance to present or receive a presentation about a potential opportunity, these conferences and events are a mainstay of building an effective network of contacts throughout the industry. Attendees will be the source of information, rumour, introductions and camaraderie amongst the business development community in health-care which assists in the interchange of assets between companies, universities and their investors.

When making appointments at partnering meetings some research is required beyond the brief description of the company given on their websites or in their brochures. This leads to a matching of the right companies to an opportunity or identifying who to meet to open contact with the right company. When this research is completed and the bookings are made the company representative will then have an agenda of contacts and an objective for each meeting planned.

In attending these events there is a need to recognize that the investment of time and money requires sufficient commitment to make adequate use of the opportunity. Ideally each company should have at least two representatives attending each meeting, one to present and the other to listen, question and record the discussions and note any agreed points or actions made during each session. These sessions vary from 15 to 30 minutes in length and rotate according to the time schedule set by the organizers of the event. Because time is limited the exchange of information needs to be well orchestrated. Over the years of a 'formula' has evolved for these encounters which in general produces a useful result. Each of the companies will have a prepared PowerPoint presentation or similar document which describes the following:

- the company background

- the purpose of the meeting

- a description of the opportunity

- features of the
  - pre-clinical data
  - market data
  - development plan

- the desired outcome

- contact details.

This presentation will typically be 10 to 20 slides in length and may be on a laptop computer and /or hard copy (it is preferable to have hard copies to hand in any case to exchange with the counterparty). This will serve the purpose of making contemporaneous notes of answers to questions on the relevant slide and to make up the take-home message. This assists both teams as the message is concise, structured and to the point. Both sides can present and, if desired, meet-up later to expand on points of interest and they can fix a meeting then and there for later at the conference, or for another date and venue. A full presentation with technical data and back-up publications can be reserved for this subsequent meeting. Less skilled practitioners unfortunately do not stick to this formula and tend to try and present their full company history and business case in 15 minutes which neither does justice to the opportunity nor permits enough time for the counterparty to reply. Proper preparation for these events is therefore highly desirable and will bring better results for both protagonists.

As mentioned above the intensity of these meetings makes them very worthwhile if handled correctly during the event but that also requires considerable post hoc management in the recording of the interaction in such a way that it can be shared with others in the company after the event. Depending on the complexity of the organization this process can be enhanced by a standard reporting template in which the contact, content and conclusion of each session can be added to an archive for distribution to relevant colleagues and then retrieved for later. It may also be included as an aspect of the transaction documentation and as a part of the corporate knowledge-base of contacts, opportunities screened, and as a measure of the amount of effort expended in the business development process. The notes made by the second and passive person in the meeting might be entered directly into a document format on computer or transcribed later with additional notes. For smaller organizations the alternative is the 'lab book' approach where each meeting is written into a hardbacked notebook which becomes a direct archive for the business development professional. This is fine for a time but the ability to recall the data on the day is limited by the number of books an individual can carry! Some form of meeting log is nevertheless required to maintain a relationship between companies, which can span many years and even many individuals before developing into a potential transaction.

The search strategy therefore needs to be tailored to the needs of the company, the resources available and the potential partners for the opportunity. The search itself may be broad-ranging or tightly focused and can be conducted passively up to a point but then must be converted into a structured discussion to establish where the potential for a transaction exists. How then to decide whether a discussion on the phone or in person should be continued, terminated or postponed? The answers to this lie in part in the profile of the opportunity generated earlier but, very importantly, the interaction will also have generated new information which may modify the inputs of the profile model. As a result it will be necessary to revisit the profile continuously throughout the search procedure in order to verify that the assumptions made were correct, that they remain correct and, that the profile itself is still relevant in the light of this new data. If for instance one of the key tenets for acquiring or licensing the product is that it will be a class leader but it is found during the search process that a different treatment modality is about to enter the market with a more attractive profile, it is time to change your mind!

Competitive intelligence

This brings into focus the need for competitive intelligence which as a specialty needs to be differentiated from market research. Market research is the study of quantitative data about a market and qualitative data in that market concerning the attitudes of customers to the products that make it up. Competitive intelligence is the acquisition of data on the activities and make-up of companies active in the market. Unlike market data, which forecast and estimate the size of a market or customer behaviour, competitive intelligence is aimed at predicting the *actions* of competitors and planning suitable counter strategies to achieve competitive advantage. It therefore adds a completely different dimension to the understanding of the market and the value of an opportunity. The search process is a way of acquiring significant competitive intelligence about companies and products which will form the medium in which your profiled opportunity will perform. Yet the search process will also open a window on to your activities for your competitors who will be able to observe your own actions and factor these into their own plans. As a result, a degree of what can be termed 'counter-intelligence thinking' needs to be incorporated into your search activities. In a counter-intuitive way despite the need to communicate your needs and desires to your audience you also need to make the information partial and privileged at the same time. This can be a difficult balancing act; on numerous occasions I've been engaged in a search process and found out much more than I had expected just by talking to the company's competitors, who through constant vigilance knew them well. Their investors, their scientists at specialist congresses are also starved of gossip and are only too willing to give you their views if asked correctly. These sources can be highly indiscreet and although biased in their views, if the information is treated with sufficient caution when fully interpreted it can often tell you a great deal more than the company would itself divulge through the trained responses of its own business development function. As a result your own people in these functions need to be briefed to protect your company information; however, as you will never be able to keep your competitors quiet, plugging all the gaps will impossible.

As the search progresses however the company will build up an impressive collection of information about an opportunity and this will accumulate into an increasingly disorganized mass of quite unrelated data. It is worthwhile therefore to sit down from time to time, either alone or with the team, and collect the information about each of the opportunities you are pursuing to match each particular portfolio need. This can be done either by having a standard question list or a template which can organize the information and assist with comparisons or, particularly in a team environment, it is useful to employ techniques such as 'mind mapping' to try and capture the body of knowledge which has accumulated and mould it into a coherent model.

Mind mapping can be achieved using a straightforward pencil-and-paper approach or several well-developed software packages which are now available such as MindManager® from Mindjet Ltd. These have the benefit of being capable of online sharing through email or used in networked sessions, perhaps including videoconferencing where personnel from different locations from the company and external sources can participate simultaneously in the collection exercise to pool the company's knowledge. Another advantage of using techniques of this kind is that the current state of completeness of the search can be evaluated for any individual opportunity or may be used on a comparative basis across opportunities. Hence the progress of the search plan can be evaluated and further questions that need to be answered noted and perhaps assigned to one of the team members to acquire.

Opening a product's profile to an independent review is also a good way of testing the potential value of an opportunity. This can avoid the risk of your internal team 'talking themselves into' pursuing a product unnecessarily. Just today I was in an investment meeting where a new formulation process was being proudly presented to a group of investors by a newly formed company. This company had been developing their product towards what they believed would be a 'proof of concept' and so become an attractive investment for venture capitalists. As the questioning by the potential investors became more

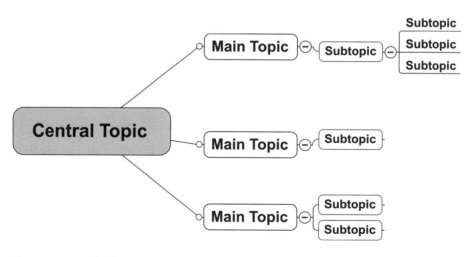

Figure 4.4   Mind mapping

detailed it soon became clear that some urgent data requirements existed on which the company had no information. The product's method of delivery was by oral administration of peptides and other large molecules such as proteins, yet the mechanism of action of the delivery for their first compound was not yet known. Furthermore, although they had observed biological activity through effects on surrogate markers, they had not yet detected the blood levels of the molecule found in the test subjects. When they were asked they volunteered that the bioavailability of the product was thought to be in the range of 5–7 per cent.

These few facts brought a torrent of questions forward from the members of the meeting with a clinical background, such as: What is the inter-patient variability in absorption? How many patients had been tested? What was the therapeutic index of the products to be tested? (This would mean that if the maximum tolerated dose were low and the bioavailability were low in most but not all patients, there would be a risk of some patients receiving potentially toxic doses of the active products!) How would the low bioavailability be applicable to biological products with a high cost of goods? It rapidly became clear that the clinical programme necessary to answer these questions and secure the needed investment would be far more costly than the company envisaged and funding would not be achieved until the questions were answered, making the presentation more than a little premature. Provoking the interest of the investors revealed gaping holes in the data which sparked the incredulity among the investors and completely altered the perception of the opportunity in a short period of time. Had this been a search candidate it would have been easy to put it aside and select an alternative until these points were resolved saving time and effort for more productive targets. It illustrates how easy it is to become blinkered to the faults of a project by being too immersed in it. As a further reflection this company had 'blown it' with these investors when instead they could have performed this challenge process with independent experts privately before going to a 'live' audience with a half-formed pitch.

Confidentiality

There will come a time, however, when the information required from a company which will permit a decision on whether or not to continue with an enquiry is of a confidential nature, such as a trade secret, some form of know-how or an as yet unfiled patent which cannot be shared without legal protection for the company divulging the information. The means to avoid this issue is by drawing up of a confidential disclosure agreement (CDA) sometimes called a non-disclosure agreement (NDA). The latter acronym may confusing in pharmaceutical markets where an NDA is also the acronym for a new drug application, thus CDA is quite often preferred to avoid confusion.

The CDA acts as anything from a simple agreement to act in good faith and not to disclose to others information obtained under its protection or to make use of the information without a licence or can become a full-blown contract in itself including definitions of the information and with subclauses affecting the rights and duties of each party and spelling out the circumstances and consequences regarding improper use of information. As this is a legal document which can be enforced by one company on another it is prudent to involve the legal department in executing such a document. It has now frequently become the case that a CDA must be negotiated and rewritten several times as unfortunately many companies have fallen into the habit of using a 'standard' CDA which has aggregated all kinds of protective clauses that have been used in the past for such agreements which are retained 'in case' they might be useful. Sadly this 'covering the backside' approach in some cases generates 20-page or more documents which are unwieldy and quite often irrelevant to the actual needs of the situation. One is tempted to believe that it would be often wiser to have different levels of 'stock' CDAs to facilitate the search process so that a 'CDA-lite' version could be executed rapidly by both sides to establish the presence or absence of a business case without undue delay. If the initial diligence proves good then a full CDA can then be established when there is a probability that the transaction will follow and will require full due diligence. Too much time is wasted in legal wrangling over irrelevant clauses over many weeks and at great cost when a simpler agreement would serve the basic needs of protecting the disclosing company's interests.

A basic CDA should contain as few clauses as possible such as:

- the names of the parties and their addresses;

- the purpose of the document for example, an evaluation of the product;

- the agreement not to disclose confidential information;

- the duration of the agreement;

- an agreement to return any exchange materials required;

- exceptions due to law;

- signatory parties.

It is also the case that companies have developed a reflex to require a CDA before there is any disclosure of information between the parties which again is time-wasting and inefficient. While it would hardly be thought professional to exchange a CDA with a company and then only share information already in the public domain, this happens frequently when people slavishly follow a pre-set procedure without thinking of the consequences. The CDA should protect only specific disclosures of truly confidential information. That said it is also possible to accidentally learn too much during the search procedure.

Another document which can be required as the search progresses is the Material Transfer Agreement (MTA) which is required when a compound needs to be provided by one company to another for the evaluation of special characteristics which are claimed, or are believed to be present in the compound. For instance, it may be that the partnering company has a specific proprietary screen or assay set up. If the partner thinks the compound will demonstrate a desired effect which would be required for their product profile but the originator company does not have the facilities to perform then the sample must be tested by the potential licensee. This is the case in many of the larger companies who have developed proprietary in-house assays of very high specificity or sensitivity which give their research an advantage over their competitors and so they will need to test every potential new compound for themselves. Within an MTA specific clauses prevent the testing company from performing other tests or modifying the sample in any way.

The reason for this is clear from a story I heard at a conference once where a scientist in one of the larger companies had received a sample under MTA from a potential partner. Another of their scientists was asked to perform the assay; however, this fellow was rather new and was not aware of the conditions of an MTA having just started at the company from a university where free experimentation was pretty normal. So he took the sample into his lab and, because he recognized the type of molecule from work he'd done before, he 'helped' his business development colleague who had been complaining that the compound was poorly soluble in water (which can prevent a compound from ever becoming a worthwhile product in the market) by altering the compound to make it water soluble with his own process. What this did of course was to make the molecule instantly extremely valuable. But, although the company now had a very valuable asset, it didn't own it. Furthermore, they couldn't use the information that the modification had permitted without disclosing the violation of the MTA to the partner which compromised them completely. Under the MTA all IP relating to the compound including any accidental inventions remains the property of the owner. In the end, I'm told, through complex negotiations it turned out that the product could be developed between the two companies and in fact may soon come to market. This story also illustrates the need for the business development group to have control over the processes during search and evaluation of compounds. The value of the intellectual property is the value of the product; without this it is only chemistry.

In other areas of the health-care business such as medical devices and diagnostics there are often parts of IP which are never patented; for instance, the know-how required in production. This know-how can be very hard to establish and even harder to evaluate. By way of example taken from another instance where I was involved, the client had taken over a company in which the main product included a technology where the active ingredients were suspended in a two-phase liquid. This was then blended by a special process which was what gave the product its special release attributes. Unfortunately, following the takeover, as a part of the cost reductions which are often needed to justify the acquisition price paid for a company, the man who had been in charge of the production process that the suspended the active ingredient was made redundant. As a consequence in the subsequent batches of the product the liquids started to separate or 'crack' after the batch was made, rendering it useless. No documentation change had been made to the process since it had been invented and so no one could explain the sudden failure. After several lost batches which resulted in a period of market withdrawal and involving great cost, the client company worked out that there must be some 'magic' in the way the product had been made before and so the production man was found and the know-how recovered, allowing the product back to the market. When the acquirer had evaluated this particular product they had looked at the IP and the production process procedures but had overlooked the know-how required to produce a stable product.

Initial due diligence

The process of due diligence in and through the search phase is an intrinsic part of the evaluation of opportunities and shows that the value of an experienced hand in guiding the criteria for the search and evaluation process is of paramount importance. Evaluation thus comes in several different forms: there are quantitative, factual, speculative and qualitative elements to an evaluation which require a degree of 'codification' and some which need a degree of 'gut-feel'. While the pharmaceutical world is full of instances where hearts have overruled heads and been right about the value of a product, and the converse situation, where products have been wilfully pursued despite the fact that all the evidence was stacked against them only to end in ignominious failure also happens, I can offer no way of helping to instil the required 'gut-feel' into others yet I shy away from the idea that everything can be reduced to some kind of quantitative algorithm.

Both methods serve their purpose in the real world of developing medicines and, after all, as the target of all medicine is the human body, which is highly variable, being a biological entity, uncertainty cannot be avoided. This uncertainty sustains the need for some 'art' within all the science that we can bring to bear.

In evaluation there are a number of factors which should be borne in mind regarding the nature of the evidence which will be reviewed. The most significant of these is the selectiveness of the data that can be acquired. Any information on early stage compounds will be bedevilled by a sheer lack of data. When a compound is new it just cannot be that all of the possible experiments needed to answer the many very necessary questions will have been performed. One example is the information on ADMET (absorption, distribution, metabolism, elimination and toxicology) for a compound. The battery of tests available for these evaluations has proliferated in the last 5 years to the point where no minimum standard of, for instance, safety is clearly accepted either by companies or regulatory agencies. The result is that few companies can afford to perform more than a sample of what is available. Data on the pharmacokinetics (PK) and pharmacodynamics (PD) of a compound need to be established in vitro, then in vivo in recognized animal models (and these may not even exist for some new classes of compound) and very possibly in human tissue models. Yet even these tests can do very little to predict the likely response across such variables as genetic difference or dietary effects and these can profoundly affect the potential of a drug (see Figure 4.5).

It has to be accepted therefore that the level of risk in early compounds is extreme and this reduces only gradually until studies in quite large populations have been tested. Consequently the evaluation of a compound or other kind of asset must be realistically limited to what it is actually possible to know at the time, and acted upon accordingly.

My own chosen method is therefore an amalgam of soft and hard features each of which cannot be directly compared or inferred one from another but can be elaborated into what I've called an 'evaluation array' (see Figure 4.6).

The idea behind this is to place alongside one another the salient features of an opportunity and reach a kind of 'sum value', recognizing that there is no way of performing a valid calculation which can discriminate between the opportunities. The idea of an array comes from the computing world where a variable in array can either be independent, dependent or variable. Although the concept of a variant variable may seem a little esoteric, let me try and explain. The independent variable in any array is the fact which stands alone,

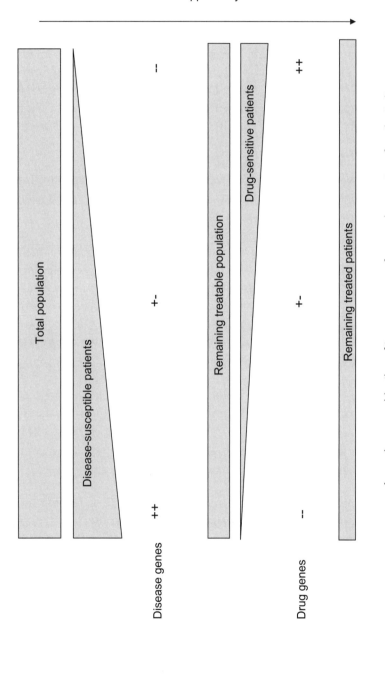

Figure 4.5 Genetic reduction of market opportunity

Arrays are grid-like calculation tools which can have many dimensions

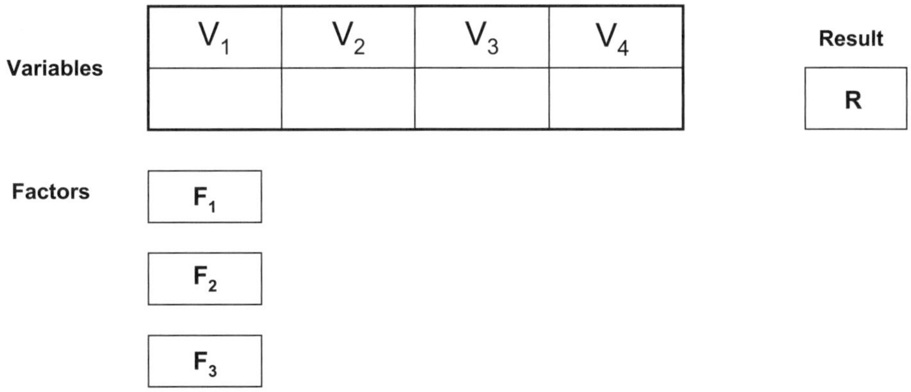

	V_1	V_2	V_3	V_4		Result
Variables						
						R

Factors	F_1

F_2

F_3

Variable 1 can be fixed, or made up of factors 1, 2, 3, or more.
Variable 2 – 'n' has the same characteristics.
So a result can be generated for different variables made up from multiple factors. The factors and variables can then be altered to see their effect.

Figure 4.6   Evaluation array

such as the incidence of the disease of interest in a particular country. If the incidence and the death rates (or sometimes the cure rate) are known then we can work out the prevalence. From this the total population which can be treated at any one time is an independent variable in the array. The treatment rate, however, is dependent on the rate of diagnosis and the compliance of the patients with therapy which can be estimated and sometimes altered by the existence of a product to treat the disease. Hence the dependent variable is made up of a number of factors which can alter over time and be influenced by actions such as product promotion. Such promotion is itself a 'variant' variable in this analysis because you can choose how much goes into this and change it at will.

The evaluation array therefore is a conceptual spreadsheet, so it can be modelled – up to a point – but because of the number of dimensions involved it needs then to be appraised by 'eyeballing' the resulting data and making a judgement about the relative worth of each piece of data and the whole 'package' of information the array describes, and then choices must be made based on this.

As pointed out above the chances of being wrong are very high in all cases due to the nature of the medical treatments. Tamar Howson, who leads business development at Bristol-Myers Squibb, made this very observation at a recent conference in London. Four out of five of the late-stage licensing deals her company had concluded in the preceding couple of years had failed to make it through the clinic. This was due to no failure in the business development process but merely reflects the nature of risk in the pharmaceutical industry.

Modelling and Valuation

Valuation

One of the most contentious issues in business development is valuation. In truth there is no method which will provide a correct value. Value can only be accurately gauged when an asset is realized. Between the invention of an idea for a product or company and the eventual sale, no matter what method is chosen to act as a surrogate for the real value, intangible elements will remain and confound the accuracy of any valuation. Even when an asset is sold the price paid may not match its expected value.

I was involved in a transaction to purchase the marketing rights from one of the biggest companies for an older product which no longer fit into their strategy. The larger company had set a floor price below which they would not sell and this was based on a multiple of the residual sales (these were continuing despite a number of years without the product being promoted). The acquiring company needed to find extra funding in order to acquire the assets. They believed that even with an upfront purchase price of $90 million plus royalties on sales of the product they would be able to revive the product's fortunes in the market by relaunching it. They were also able to add two new indications through more clinical development and consequently their model showed that there would be sufficient value to repay the financing costs and yield a substantial profit. By raising the required capital the company went on to complete the transaction. As luck would have it, the acquiring company became so cash rich because of this acquisition and because of raising more money to fund the clinical developments that it became the target of a takeover. Yet less than 2 years later those same assets which it had bought for $90 million were sold on to another company for only $19 million by the new owner. Intrinsically it was still the same product and in the same market, but for the people making the valuation second time around, there was a very different view of the product's worth. This example illustrates several features of the valuation process but it underscores the most significant which are the *assumptions* which underlie the model.

Essentially valuation is dependent on a qualitative and quantitative model which is made up of a series of assumptions. Each of these is based on data and observations of the market which are then mixed with the prejudices, guesses, hopes and ambitions of the modellers. In many respects the modeller and the model the surrogate for the asset, and so the method used to build the model has a major effect on the outcome. One way to try and overcome the bias and risk that this exercise brings is, where possible, to have more than one modeller using a different method to create their model. In this way the different models created can cross-check each other. If the results of the different models are similar there is some hope that an approximately true result will not be far away. Naturally if the results of the models are wildly different the reasons for this may become apparent and corrections maybe applied. In navigation either at sea or in the air, a similar method is used for position fixing. The navigator will take not one or two but, if possible, several bearings from objects on the horizon from which they can plot as intersecting lines on a chart to find their position. However, the lines most often do not meet at a convenient point and will often leave a small usually triangular gap known as a 'cocked hat' (see Figure 5.1) especially when three bearings are used in which the vessel is likely to be found. The bigger the triangle the less sure the navigator is about their location which, if the triangle also contains, say, a reef, may become a problem. So to refine the result of their cocked-hat position-fixing method, the more bearings the navigator has the better.

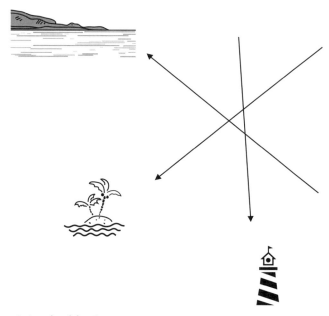

Figure 5.1   A 'cocked hat'

In a similar fashion GPS, the global positioning system, uses many satellites to achieve an accurate result (see Figure 5.2). When only a few are above the horizon the position fix is perhaps to the nearest kilometre or so, but if there are eight or more satellites, positions can be fixed to a few metres. So it is clear that whether one modeller is used and several methods, or many modellers and many methods, relying on only a single attempt no matter how complex would be the most risky approach to modelling.

Approaches to modelling

In health-care markets a few basic approaches are in common use and each has its merits and drawbacks yet as the complexity increases there is a greater likelihood that the results obtained may be influenced by minor alterations in the assumptions. The first and very common method I shall refer to is 'top down', which is when the model is created using the sales figures from existing products in a market as the definition of the market itself. An example: if a new ACE inhibitor product enters the ACE inhibitor market it might reasonably be expected to take market share from the existing products unless somehow it were to be used in a completely different set of patients with another disease. Suppose the market were made up of five products. If the new product has better features than three of the other products, and they represent 50 per cent of all sales in that market, then the new product might be expected to take half

Figure 5.2   GPS triangulation

of the sales of each of the three over 5 years, eventually achieving a 25 per cent market share (see Figure 5.3).

This top down method is quite reasonable and fairly robust but, as can be seen from the example, it is very simplistic in its assumptions. It would only take the introduction of new products from another class of compounds (which also affect high blood pressure or congestive heart failure in a similar way) that produce better effects to reduce the market opportunity for ACE inhibitors. This would alter the value of the ACE inhibitor market dramatically and even a 25 per cent share might be worth much less than anticipated. As a result of the need to take this into account the next level of model must include all the other players in the market.

Carrying on with the ACE inhibitor example, this then means all products in each of the clinical indications in which ACE inhibitors are used must be incorporated in the model. This will mean including not only the 'approved indications' for which the products are licensed for use but any other clinical uses. This introduces both quantitative and qualitative elements to the model and requires considerably more information if we are to have a hope of its being accurate. Typically for pharmaceuticals a quantitative meausure may be a count of the amount of each product sold by price, by units and by weight. The reason for these measures is to establish the overall value of the market. The number of dose units establishes the number of times patients use the product and the total, or aggregate weight in kilos of a molecule that is included in many different forms such as tablets, capsule or injections, can establish which product is selling the most out of a group of competitors. Another quantitative

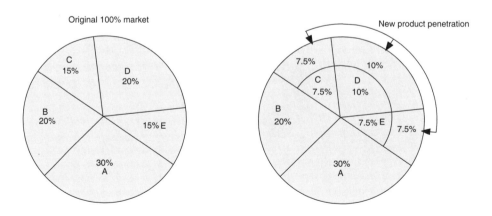

Figure 5.3   Market share penetration

measure is counts of prescriptions which give an estimate of what disease the products are used for. This can also show the effectiveness of the promotional effects of the company. Each of these elements is interlinked and gives substance to the model.

However, within this newfound structure there is a problem in that the sales figures by value, units and weight are usually collected at source and so are close to census data that is, representing nearly the whole universe of products sold. The prescription data, however, are collected by sample which means that the data are only a representation of the total universe of prescriptions and so are open to a much wider interpretation and error. Many years ago, I launched a product in the UK and became a victim of this anomaly. The product was also being studied by the headquarter function of the company I was working for. They believed that available prescription data were as accurate as the sales data but, unfortunately for them and for me, among the sample of doctors recording the prescriptions in the UK was one man who had a dispensing practice. He had made our new product his product of choice thanks to our persuasive representative and so all of his prescriptions for new and switch patients received our new product. However, the market research sample, including his data, was then projected up to a 'national equivalent' and the headquarter researchers came looking to me for the sales of the new product. According to the prescription data it had a 7 per cent market share the first 6 months after launch, while its sales were less than 1 per cent!

Complex models

More complex models than the previous approach include the underlying epidemiological data for the disease. These data too in most countries are based not on census reporting but on sampled data. As a result the number of patients thought to have a disease is expressed as a rate per 10,000 or 100,000 depending on the sample size and the projection factor, which can magnify the margin of error. At a national level, such a model serves very well for policy planning purposes; however, the danger for the modeller lies in taking this approximation of the real world created from samples and using it as the basis for a detailed financial model.

While this criticism serves to emphasize the fragility of the data there is frequently no other or better alternative. Questions concerning approximation are, however, vital in the context of a valuation where forecasts need to be turned into cash. Using epidemiological data or algorithms and applying them to fundamental datasets can give the appearance of a very realistic or indeed surreal view of the dynamics of the market. The underlying trends may give a worthwhile indication of the growth or decline, yet the more surrealism that is injected into these models the greater is the danger that they will be taken to be a true representation of the world rather than what they are, which is just a fallible model.

The greatest peril in modelling is that in order to achieve the sensitivity desired to engender trust in a model it may become prey to outlying data points and freak occurrences. Markets may be changed by political or economic events and climatic changes referred to as acts of God or 'force majeure'. Because these events are by their nature unpredictable they cannot be modelled and lurk behind spreadsheets to confound the unwary. Even relatively benign events, such as a change in reimbursement in a major market, can have dramatic effects on pharmaceutical markets. The addition of diagnostic procedures to a reimbursement plan has often been seen to drive up the number of diagnoses dramatically; an example being in the diabetes market, which increased sharply when many countries decided that the economic burden of the disease on society far outweighed the cost of diagnosis, treatment and reimbursing glucose stick use.

An improvement in sensitivity in a diagnostic procedure can have similar effects. The introduction of simple cholesterol testing at point of care has been a major contributor to fuelling the market for 'statin' treatments for mild hypercholesterolemia and added billions to the market for preventative cardiovascular medicines. Acceptance by health-care authorities of the statistical relevance of treatment of both raised blood pressure and cholesterol has been a significant source of pharmaceutical growth. The proof of the value of those interventions has though only recently become available, as the population statistics including the changes in major cause of death seems now to be bearing out the model that preventative treatment will reduce deaths from coronary heart disease. This is now clearly shown to be the case despite the confounding coincidence of a reduction in smoking and improved diet and exercise.

It should not be forgotten that models as a function of their simplicity are therefore a fiction and it is easy to come to disparate conclusions if the model's parameters are interpreted differently. In establishing a model for transaction it is therefore important to derive a model using a similar methodology to the one the counterparty has used or if not similar in method, one which achieves congruent results. Hence the approaches need to be based on, as far as possible, contiguous datasets. Suppliers of census and sample data include IMS, DataMonitor and their affiliates and subsidiaries such as Scott Levin and Walsh Systems.

What then is the right model? What degree of sophistication or otherwise is justified to produce a robust basis for valuation? Factors affecting the answer include the following:

- *Timing*, if you have very little time to create the model then complexity should be avoided.

- *Data*, if the data available are scarce or untrustworthy – which may be because the collection method is vague, or the collection is discontinuous – wider parameters need to be accepted for variance in the model.

- The *audience*, this differs according to business culture and particularly in the USA 'hard numbers' are required on every available occasion, while in Europe and in Japan more reliance is put on interpretation as data sources tend to be less robust. US companies and financial institutions put great store in having a quantitative model including as much data as possible to 'mimic' the market. To European eyes this reliance on quantitative modelling can seem obsessive yet like it or not, if you're counterparty is American a solid model is a prerequisite to a partnering discussion.

More complex models will therefore include not only data on the sales of products and the number of patients in the market but the number of prescribing physicians, the number of representative calls made by your own and competing companies, prescribing policy and reimbursement trends, competitive products entries and the like. The result of such a model is an exquisitely sensitive tool which can be used as the basis for forecasting the potential of a product, the markets or a patient population. The next step is therefore to produce a forecast. This in itself brings another difficult choice of method as there are two fundamental paths to following in forecasting. The most usual is to look at a model and from the conditions decide or derive an initial estimate of the potential of the product. This might be 0.5 per cent of the market or maybe 1 per cent in the first year. Following this and the other assumptions in the model an estimate can be made of the next year and onwards from there to produce a sales line for maybe 5 years during which time the major parameters of the model such as the population size are likely to hold good. Typically two or more other forecasts are produced with slightly differing assumptions on the influence of the key drivers in the model to generate a low, medium and high forecast line which expression represents degrees of confidence in the model and its resultant forecast. This method is rational and quite satisfactory for most purposes; however, in pharmaceutical markets where treatments have not been available before and where the model characteristics have little or no precedents another method may be more appropriate. This is sometimes referred to as an heuristic or 'prophesy' method. The central feature of this method is to set a target figure for say the fifth year and then test the possibility of that number being achieved within the constraints of the model. Let's assume the target has been set for €100 million turnover in the fifth year. That figure can be derived from a number of units being used at a given price. In order for this to happen a specific number of patients will have needed to have been diagnosed and treated with the product and then to have completed a course of treatment of a given length. A given number of doctors must have been contacted and converted to the use of the product. This logical sequence allows questions to be addresses such as: 'How likely is it that this can have occurred within the model constraints?' It is often very useful to graph each one of the components of the model to see if there is a visual continuity in the development of the figures. If a sudden jump is required in the model affecting one or more of the parameters it is likely that the target figures will be unattainable under those assumptions. This leads to the conclusion that either the target number is wrong or the model is wrong. It naturally follows that this method can be used to explain doubts in the expectation of counterparties and their forecast and models and become an integral part of the negotiation process. So-called 'challenge targets' internally set by the company can be deconstructed using this method too.

However, before that point is reached it is advisable to subject the finished model and the forecast to what is referred to as 'stress' or 'sensitivity' testing. This process is achieved by taking the model and varying each of the parameters or assumptions to estimate the sensitivity of the model to that single parameter or any other logical combination of parameters. If the model is seen to produce extreme results through only a small shift in one parameter or another, it is vital that the underlying dataset for the parameter is as robust as possible. If for instance market penetration is a function of representative call rate, the quality of calls or the type of doctor being detailed, the product may also be the issue of critical importance. A closer understanding of the dynamics of this component might be needed and additional market research must be conducted.

New product issues

New products are notoriously difficult to model and one of the most sensitive factors in such models is the product's proposed price. Consequently qualitative research is most frequently required to derive pricing models for the market and the product. Many times products have been launched with entirely false expectations of what the potential might be because the price point in the market has been misunderstood.

To address this issue there are various ways to estimate price. The most obvious is to use an existing product as the benchmark. In interviews or focus groups doctors can be challenged to estimate the likelihood of their paying a particular price for the product. The profile will be read out to the doctors and they must choose where in a scale of prices they would feel justified in prescribing the product. An alternative is to read out the profile description and then ask if they feel it should cost more or less than each of a number of reference products. This technique can be particularly useful where doctors have little knowledge of the actual cost of products, since a sense of the value can be established by relating it to different attributes than the price in isolation which, taken alone, can sometimes generate misleading answers. For instance the doctor may not consider a product too expensive for herself at €5.00 per month, but if the patients in her list are poor she might choose to say the product is too expensive on their behalf. As an alternative, relating the medical benefits of the product profile to other well-known products can elicit less guarded responses which will be guided by more pertinent issues.

By following these procedures a model of known reliability will be created and its dependence on the various contributing factors that make it up will be known. Forecasts will have been generated for the model and tested against the limitations checks of the model in its various states and now be ready to produce a valuation.

What then is meant by valuation beyond having generated the sales line from the model? Firstly the costs associated with the product need to be superimposed on the forecasts to generate an estimate of the financial contribution; the sales less the cost of making the sales gives the gross margin and following from this the gross margin less the cost of goods gives the contribution. The cumulative contribution of the product can then be estimated over time (the cost of sales are not constant as they will be higher at launch and then reduce thereafter throughout the forecast period). It is worth mentioning that there is a wide variation in the launch costs required, for example, between hospital and primary care products. Similar wide variances occur between the continuing costs of medicines for acute conditions like those designed for a short duration of use, such as antibiotics (where physicians may choose from several comparable products), and the costs of sales for long-term illnesses or chronic medications which generate repeat prescriptions (where the products are less likely to require constant visits by representatives to stimulate continued use by the physicians). Advice from experienced marketing staff is of great value in gauging the amount of expenditure on sales and marketing required to achieve a successful launch and to maintain sales growth of different types of product and in different kinds of markets such as the cyclic markets like antihistamines, travellers' vaccines and the like where annual promotional 'bursts' of activity are needed.

Another factor which plays a part might be high cost of goods as this can drive the in-market price for a product to a point where market penetration becomes limited and this is particularly so where patients are making the purchase or making a significant co-payment. This is accentuated even more if the product is for a disease which is more inconvenient than painful or life threatening and price elasticity is low. At the company level in the context of a portfolio, a product which has a low margin or is resource hungry will have a value impaired by comparison with more typical products as it may take cash away from other operations and depress earnings unless the volume of sales that it generates can compensate at the level of cash flow by passing the contribution threshold. There is therefore a balance to be met between the cash the product brings in and its overall effect on the company. The value will again have to be calculated as an absolute amount and in relation to the portfolio to give a true estimate of its value. In the absolute estimation a discounted cash flow method is most frequently used to decide whether a product will produce profits based on its assumptions in the model. The most frequently used result from this cash flow analysis is the expression of the 'net present value' of the project.

Measures of value

I was sitting in a conference one morning recently alongside one of the investment directors of a medium-sized venture fund whom I know. We were listening to another panel of investors, bankers and company partnering executives talking about the state of the market and the opportunity for an initial public offering (IPO) versus a trade sale to a big company. The alliance director from one of the bigger pharmaceutical companies had just offered the opinion from the panel that in a competitive market it was sometimes worth making a high upfront payment to secure a key piece of IP. Another of the panellists asked him how he judged the monetary value on the bid to which his answer was, 'Enough to make sure we win.' I asked my friend from the venture capital fund how they made their investment valuations and if it was more scientific, to which his reply was, 'No one knows how to value these companies – we all just guess!' To a large extent this is absolutely true. It's really just a matter of how you guess and who believes you.

Different value perspectives

When it comes to valuing an asset, whether it's a company, a product, a development project, a technology, a manufacturing method or an IP position, the value has to be seen in the context of whoever is looking at it. The relationship between the asset and its value can only be established from the points of view of the buyer and the seller. In either case at base there will be an 'absolute' value which might be derived from the cost of producing the asset added to which will be the 'potential' value based upon a forecast, in other words what the asset may be able to generate in terms of future monetary returns. Unfortunately for the person doing the valuation, a brilliant idea may have cost nothing but be worth millions, while a project which has cost millions to develop may end up being worth nothing. Consequently much more needs to be considered before arriving at an expression of appropriate value

The first question to ask is: Who is the acquirer? What is their motivation? How well funded are they? What risk tolerance do they have? These and other questions need to be answered en route to achieving an asset valuation. Moreover these questions must be addressed at the particular time of the valuation as the context of the valuation is vital to the result. A product which is a first-to-market product opening up a new area of medicine may be very valuable; conversely a product which succeeds and surpasses the first-to-market may be even more valuable as the market will have been established and any 'room for improvement' identified opening the opportunity for the newcomer. Thus the circumstances surrounding the judgement of value are frequently the critical deciding factors, and hindsight is a luxury yet to come. When many a deal is first announced it is viewed with horror by financial analysts in the light of what they knew about the company at the time of execution, but they are sometimes forced to recant a year later when the deal is revealed as giving a huge advantage to the buyer because of developing features not apparent to the outside world. Conversely the opposite happens just as frequently with the result that another CEO leaves to 'spend more time with his family'.

New ventures

Many as the issues are surrounding the valuation of an existing company, these are accentuated to almost grotesques propositions in the case of new ventures.

This could be a new company or an internal project within a company for a new business area. There will be problems around the lack of data about the market, and uncertainties about the technical feasibility of the technology or the functional performance of the product in a treatment setting. A good example of some of the key issues affecting new ventures is one I ran into while in investing. This particular product had been developed for the treatment of head and neck cancer using photodynamic therapy, a procedure which involved injecting the patient with a product which was taken up preferentially by cancer cells in the surface layers of the mouth and throat. These layers are prone to cancers because of their exposure to environmental carcinogens. These areas would then be exposed to laser light of a specific frequency which would activate the product and destroy the cancer cells. The product had been developed at some considerable cost and in practice had been shown to produce effective removal of enough of the cells to provide a medium-term solution to the disease by preventing the continued runaway growth of the tumour. It could be used again and again to palliate the patients' condition. Therefore the company had an effective therapy for a serious disease where few other treatments provide worthwhile long-term benefits.

In theory therefore this should have been a very valuable product, but the company had had enormous difficulty in raising funds. There were many reasons for this but one of the most telling was that that the experimental use of this kind of therapy had never been successfully converted into a regular treatment before. In part this was because earlier photodynamic therapies that had been tried were plagued by side effects (these products stayed in the bloodstream for too long after the treatment session and because sunlight also contains light of the frequency of the laser light, patients were required to stay indoors during daylight for weeks). Because of this none of the medical reviewers had a good opinion of this method and this affected the view of the financial analysts as they could not find any positive references in the medical literature or any data for an existing market for the treatment of head and neck cancer. These factors contributed to the product receiving inadequate funds to conduct extensive clinical trials which further reinforced its negative image. In the end the product did come to market but has yet to succeed as it lacks the funds for the education and promotion which it would require to become better accepted.

This story demonstrates the difficulties of valuation in this sort of situation. It is extremely hard to achieve where there is no comparator product, no existing treatment which can show the extent of the opportunity and so also no precedent for pricing. When there is little in the way of solid fact on which to base a valuation it is difficult for potential investors to judge whether the potential of a product will exceed the investment required to bring it to market and, naturally, this leads to many products being without funds and undeveloped. Investors will err on the side of caution when they do not understand a model or distrust its data.

Steady state

This is the most comfortable situation for a forecaster is that when a steady state exists; there is usually sufficient history to obey the statistical rules of 'two periods of back data to permit one period of forecast' with a reasonable amount of confidence. A steady state does not have to imply a flat performance of a product; it could be that due to population increase there is steady growth, or that due to an increase in competition there is a steady erosion of market share and a decline. In such a situation it is reasonable to use the forecast of sales as the basis for valuation and to use the discounted cash flow method or even more simply a multiple of the total sales. Obviously the direction of the forecast will then affect the multiple used commonly being closer to one times with a declining sales pattern and two to three times for flat sales or a modest growth. When a product is performing well multiples may be higher but this can also be affected by there being a premium being paid for such an attractive asset above the absolute sales. Consequently multiples of five or six times sales are not unknown where growing assets are being traded.

The question of why a seller would choose to dispose of such a product becomes an important one. In a consolidating market the most usual cause is the forced divestment of assets during a merger or acquisition where agencies such as the Federal Trade Commission or the anti-competitive activities arm of the European Commission must rule on the combination of portfolios between prospective partners to ensure that a monopolistic position or market dominance does not result from the merger or acquisition and so disadvantage the consumer.

Buying or selling

Notwithstanding the basis for the value, an overriding issue in valuation is whether the person making the valuation is buying or selling. To use a familiar example: when you are selling a house you put a significantly higher value on your own property than you would if you were seeking to buy it. In the biopharmaceutical market assets also have different values according to the motivation of the seller. This emotional component of a sale will often have a greater effect on the price that will be paid than the history or the predicted sales. It is also important to understand who approached whom with the proposal to buy or to sell. A potential acquirer may make the first move, yet this may sometimes stimulate the potential seller either to have a higher expectation of value or, if they are unsure, to seek competitive bids to find a better offer than the initial approach. In company acquisitions the notions of 'friendly' and 'hostile' bids are usually widely separated in terms of value. Boards of companies receiving 'hostile' offers are often seen to respond in the press with protestations that the offer 'grossly undervalues' the company and its assets. They hope to stimulate competitive bids which will force improvements to the original offer, leading to a process which adjusts the value of the offers until the bid succeeds or fails.

If, however, a seller puts an asset up for sale in the absence of an existing bid there is an element of 'fishing' for a value as was seen in 2006 with the divestment of the family-owned stake in Serono. This stake was originally discussed in the financial press as having an expected value of 'around 15 billion Swiss francs' and yet it was later withdrawn from sale as none of the potential suitors for the company could justify that price to their own shareholders. In the end the stake was acquired by Merck Kgaa from Germany for a more modest 11 billion Swiss francs which represents a CHF 4 billion difference between the 'bid' and 'offer' prices – or around 30 per cent!

Expectations of value can be accurate, ambitious, mistaken or just downright cheeky but when the game is started if there is to be a sale, the buyer and the seller will have to find common ground. It is therefore prudent, when entering into the process, to consider a wider range of factors than purely a financial calculation. When I am asked to assist in the buying or selling of assets between companies among the first considerations I take into account are the timing, the motive, the motivation and the commitment to close the transaction. These must be satisfied before we select the type of buyer or partner to be approached. A symmetry and alignment of interests between the parties is very often pivotal in achieving (and defining) success.

Enterprise value

An enterprise value of a product or company is probably the most common benchmark for valuation in that it represents the sum of the values of an asset, for a product these might be sales, IP rights, manufacturing capacity, inventory and trademarks. Each of these can be assigned a nominal value and be adjusted for risks due to competition, market growth and the like. The enterprise value of a company can similarly be considered as the sum of all its assets. Where the company has shares traded publicly, equity analysts are continually making assessments of the 'fundamental' value of the company compared to the price in the market and seeking to find cases where the stock price is higher or lower and so where trading opportunities exist. However, an enterprise value is only an expression of the sum of the assets and liabilities at that time and so may not be directly related to the value that an acquirer, as opposed to a share purchaser would put on the company. It is a fair gauge of the value of the core assets but not their price in an acquisition market.

Strategic value

The strategic value of an asset is much more the expression of its potential worth in a particular set of circumstances. This might be the case for an otherwise excellent product currently languishing in the hands of a company that is too small and lacks the resources to promote it properly or, conversely, a large company whose concentration on other products in their portfolio causes the product to be neglected. This kind of product might thrive in the hands of a different company with the opportunity and desire to market the product more effectively. In this situation the value of the product to the owner will only be what they can make of it alone while a suitor company might see the chance to make a great deal more through the addition of their own capabilities. An entrepreneurial approach to such an asset might lead to an acquisition bid for the product or for the company; alternatively, it might result in a licensing transaction where combining resources results in an increase in performance which is shared between the partners. Strategic value comes about from the matching of an asset to the most appropriate resource base to maximize the asset value. This is one of the most powerful drivers of the business development process.

The way to estimate strategic value in the financial sense, in other words the premium paid beyond the enterprise value, is probably the valuation issue which is least amenable to any form of method or systematic analysis. Although previous transactions from external benchmarking or from the company's own experience may give some kind of lead, even if there is true comparability between the benchmark and the valuation subject, differences in market conditions from one day to the next will often have major influences on the price of an asset. The acquisition of Hexal by Novartis' Sandoz generic division in 2006 was widely criticized at the time as being too costly, yet immediately thereafter Teva bought Ivax to re-establish their market position among generic manufacturers which had become threatened by the creation of the Sandoz–Hexal link up. The price that Teva had to pay for Ivax was significantly more than they would have been expected to pay before the Hexal deal had re-benchmarked strategic pricing in the generic sector and sparked a round of consolidation acquisitions as each of the market leaders vied for the remaining companies to shore up their respective market shares. It should be noted that Ivax was willing to sell to Teva. What was the reason for the high price for Hexal? Almost certainly this was because Teva had also been bidding for it. Sandoz pre-empted a Teva acquisition by making an irresistible offer to Hexal's owners. This kind of bidding was repeated over Pliva later in the year with Barr Laboratories winning out after raising their offer three times bearing out the elasticity in strategic asset valuation particularly in competitive or auction bids.

Redemption value

When assets are put up for sale voluntarily, or sometimes involuntarily such as during a company liquidation, the valuation methods that are used tend to be more rational than the bidding for strategic assets and more often than not achieve less value for the vendor. In a case of this kind, contrary to the adage, the sum of the parts is actually less than the whole as the individual components are worth less alone than when valued together. Liquidations in particular normally operate under the further constraint of a time pressure and so administrators are more likely to accept a solid bid for an asset even if it is lower than the theoretical valuation might indicate. Similarly an asset's value may be impaired by unwillingness of its owner to continue providing funds for it if a portfolio review has decided that the asset is no longer a part of the core group of products which will be the drivers of growth for the company. If a divestiture is likely it should be executed rapidly as holding on to such an asset in order to obtain the best price may not be in the best interests of the company's finances if it must maintain the value by maintaining expenditure on the asset.

Another consideration which affects the value of an asset is the 'currency' that is used to pay for it: cash, equity or goodwill. Equity in place of cash can either be a compelling offer or quite the opposite. On many occasions when evaluating the value of a potential acquisition target the value of a 'cash bid' compared to the headline value that other companies were prepared to offer in the form of shares in their own company made poor comparison. The acquisition of Agouron by Warner-Lambert in 1999 was one of several deals at the time which were funded by an offer of stock of the acquiring company.

Agouron's acquisition had a headline value of $2.1 billion and set the pace for small company buy-out expectations for later deals. I was then evaluating the potential for a non-equity offer for companies in this sector, yet the valuation we reached was barely more than $1 billion when denominated in real money. In other circumstances offers have been made using stock in which the target company, on reviewing the offer, finds it has no real faith in the persisting value of the stock that it has been offered. This can lead to outright dismissal of the bid or may require a considerable increase in the number of shares demanded to compensate for the perceived lack of substance. Proffering or accepting a stock offer in these circumstances relies on equity analysts' providing a continuing positive opinion of the merged companies' future valuation to deliver shareholder value and this after all is the final denominator. As a shareholder the investor needs to be able to sell their shares at a higher value than the pre-merger price.

Structure

What stems from this discussion of these factors is the realization that value can be viewed from a myriad of different perspectives, angles and directions, whether it's buying or selling, solicited or unsolicited bids, cash or stock and the timing of the payments to name but a few.

The structure of a transaction can be as much a means to capture the value as the aggregate cash equivalent, it's all in the 'optics' or how people see things. In everyday life we normally buy small assets outright for cash and we defer the payment for other, often larger, purchases by means of credit cards, instalment purchase or by means of a mortgage arrangement. In the same way an acquisition or licensing of an asset can be structured to reflect the value it has at the present moment and bring further rewards when and where the asset is likely to appreciate, through the milestones of its future value. It is worth noting here that with the concept of future value there is a need to accept a degree of risk and this may be reflected in the absolute value by making it smaller or permitting a higher value to stand but mitigating this to some degree by structuring the transaction in a way which can limit financial exposure over time.

To take a simple case, a pharmaceutical product which is in development may have a tremendous potential value if it reaches the market, but it will have to pass many hurdles before it can generate sales and repay an investment. There are sophisticated risk assessment models which have been produced by Tufts University in the USA and these have become accepted as an industry standard for valuations of products through the various stages of development. These 'Tufts' or 'DiMasi' (named after the originator) numbers estimate the probability of success – and conversely the likelihood of failure – at each stage of the development process. If such a product is being acquired it would be prudent to limit the exposure of the acquirer by factoring the risk component into the price paid by staging the total amount into what are referred to as milestone payments. These payment thresholds are typically associated with the clinical events recognized as decisive hurdles on the pathway to market. Although the numbers are adjusted from time to time by the Tufts authors, the correlation of risk to development stage is broadly as follows:

- Preclinical: 10 per cent chance of success.

- Phase I ('human volunteer' or 'first entry into man' studies): 28 per cent chance of success.

- Phase II (safety and dose ranging studies): 50 per cent chance of success.

- Phase III (efficacy and comparative studies): 70 per cent chance of success.

These numbers are variously interpreted and are given as either the chance of success or the probability of failure. However, as these numbers are calculated differently, although they should not be used synonymously, they frequently are. Another view which is quite often taken by investors is that the later stages should have an 'allowance' factor for regulatory issues which go beyond the purely scientific, such as the relative performance of a product versus one already on the market, which may be insufficient to justify approval for marketing. As a rule of thumb, however, they serve the purpose of acting as a caution. Executives in early-stage companies are sometimes over-eager in their beliefs that their products are advanced because they have entered the clinic and are being tested in man, although a compound has come a long way by this stage it still has a highly perilous part of its journey ahead of it (see Figure 5.4).

There is also an intrinsic risk of a product being withdrawn after it has been approved for marketing. Typically this risk is at its peak in the first 3 years on the market as the number of patients in the general population exposed to the product rapidly increases and less frequent adverse events come to light. The risk of removal is, however, relatively very small and would usually be considered a normal business risk unless there is a history of failures among products of the same class. This has recently been highlighted by the discovery of an association of adverse cardiac events with COX_2 inhibitors and then

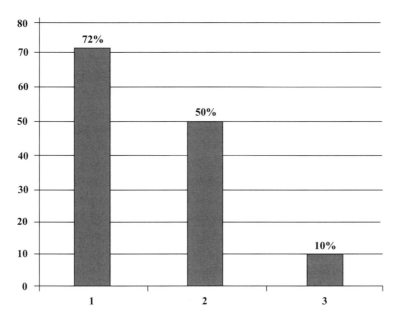

Figure 5.4   Probability of failure

the same was noted with NSAID painkiller products as both affect the COX_2 receptor and consequently seem to have some tendency to increase the risk of heart attacks in some patients. This led to the withdrawal of Merck & Co's Vioxx product, despite its having safely dosed millions of patients, to protect the few susceptible patients.

When these risk-related factors are applied to the structure of a licensing transaction it is typically reflected in an initial payment followed by later, and sometimes ascending, series of payments following successful completion of each the clinical stages, and the safety database of the product increases in size up until the product is marketed. After this it is usual to include a schedule of royalty payments which provide the originator company with a share of the product's success in the market. This structure serves the purpose of limiting risk. As the criteria for success at each milestone are achieved, value is added to the product and by deferring the payments the cost of financing the transaction is also reduced as each part of the full cost does not have to be paid until the associated risk has been dissipated and the value up-tick has been established. If however the product fails to achieve the milestone, the licensor is not liable for further payments. This general structure is therefore the most commonly found in licensing deals for early-stage and development-level products and because the risk is shared the eventual value of the deal can be substantial compared to a single early payment. In the case of product acquisitions by contrast all the risk is assumed immediately by the purchaser as a result acquisitions are often associated with marketed products where the risk has been all but eliminated. Here the overall value of an acquisition is lower and the rationale for this is that the level of risk is reduced to the commercial component but the cost is immediate and entire. A licensing transaction by comparison structurally accounts for the scientific risk by limited payments in the initial stages and accommodates for the commercial risk by means of a royalty which is performance based. As market forecasts are very often optimistic the likelihood of paying the full amount suggested by the deal terms in many cases is quite low. Where the product does become a blockbuster (commonly accepted to mean more than $1 billion in annual sales) the royalty paid will be an appropriate reward for the scientific success being converted into market success.

Combining these elements into a transaction with appropriate and symmetrical sharing of risk and reward constitutes a primary focus of business development and presents a significant challenge. The valuation components must be arranged in such a way as to reward the seller (or licensor) and protect the acquirer (or licensee) in a way which captures the inherent risks in the scientific sense and the commercial risk in the financial and marketing senses. This means rationalizing the views of all the various constituencies within both of the companies and finding the best and most workable solution. These structures are suitable to transactions between commercial companies, but what of licenses between companies and academic institutions? Here the structural elements need to address a different set of drivers for value.

Universities in particular have moved from being solely centres of basic research towards a focus of product generation as a means to acquire wealth for the institution. This movement was spearheaded by the Massachusetts Institute of Technology who have pioneered practices in technology transfer with the intention of supplementing the institute's endowment and has had a heavy emphasis on health care. Other universities the world over have not been slow to follow this model and have initiated similar programs seeing health-care biotechnology in particular as a means to capture some of the value in their research. A great many companies have been started as spin-outs of university-generated technologies with the university itself retaining significant equity stakes in each of the companies and providing business development support to the companies in at least the early stages and sometimes through a related business school. This basic public finance serves as a source of products, technologies and research platforms for the pharmaceutical, and other, industries, but also gives a different aspect to the process of valuation of biomedical assets. The search for truly analytical means for a solution to the valuation problem seems to come naturally to the academic scene and has stimulated considerable research to try and substantiate the various commonly employed methods. However, from a practical perspective the utility of these models is limited due their being originated in the absence of a truly commercial partner in the valuation process, this skews the approach more toward maximization of financial return. A university has little or no commercial agenda and so lacks a strategic component in the valuation method, with the result that the valuation is theoretical and not what someone else would actually pay. Dealing with universities, or indeed working from a university, can be challenging from a number of points of view in that a university's technology transfer group frequently has limited access to market data and few resources to conduct qualitative or quantitative market research. As a result there can be markedly different assumptions of a market's potential and very different expectations of the economics of a product within it and how this should drive the structure of the transaction required to license it.

Structuring for Value CHAPTER 6

The choice of deal structure, as has been outlined in the previous chapter, is extremely important in realizing value from the transaction. The simple examples set out before reflected the needs of a 'plain vanilla' licensing deal (named after the ice cream which has no added sprinkles or decoration). However, there will always be a need for other structures to address more complex situations. This chapter will deal with the main types of structure found in the pharmaceutical industry; acquisitions, licenses and joint ventures. Each of these may take place in a wide variety of contexts and can be used to satisfy various objectives. In the research environment there will be a range of relationships between fee-for-service research contracts, where there is no assignment of rights between the parties, through to collaborative research where the parties may apportion intellectual property (IP) rights according to their needs or this might alternatively may be constructed as a true joint-venture in which there is co-ownership of the resultant IP and joint commercial exploitation. Moving forward to a product or clinical development context, a similar range of relationships can exist but may also include a division of labour and a transfer of rights between the parties for onward licensing to a dedicated development house that takes no role in the commercialization. This is unlike an integrated pharmaceutical company which may in-license a product at an early stage, develop and then market it. At the point of commercialization the opportunity exists to share rights to a product where the ownership may be retained yet there is a sharing of the sales effort and rewards which may be divided again between licensees in different territories or perhaps also different indications (see Figure 6.1).

The extent to which a product can be shared really depends on the scale of the economics involved and the relative sizes of the parties. This will also reflect the culture of the companies which will also depend on the portfolio and their sales penetration abilities. Even a large multinational will have greater or lesser strengths across the world and could choose to partner a product for one geographical regional market or another to maximize their return through the best utilization of their resources. Individual subsidiaries nevertheless have to

Figure 6.1   Distribution of licences

obey the dynamics of their own markets as well as trying to implement a global brand strategy, after all the opportunity for an antibiotic will vary according to the prevalence of disease and patients' access to medical care.

The full array of possibilities will not, however, be followed by any particular company in the normal course of business and so for the purposes of this book the structures described will be grouped under main headings of 'Licences', 'M&A' and 'Others', always accepting that special circumstances may well require atypical solutions. In health-care markets the most frequent transaction type occurring in pharmaceutical business development is the product licence. This may be an out-licensing or an in-licensing but it should be noted that it is sometimes necessary to conduct one or more additional preparatory in-licensing deals prior to undertaking an out-licensing deal. The reasons for this are that freedom to operate needs to be established for the selected asset before you offer to license a product of your own. In order to achieve this it can be necessary to take a licence to technology from a university or inventor who owns intellectual property which dominates your product and so requires a de-blocking licence to grant freedom to operate. In the case where IP exists which could affect the rights of the licensee these so-called de-blocking licences may be taken to secure limited rights to an enabling technology, a process or similar encumbrance. A licence of this kind is frequently non-exclusive

Valuation components

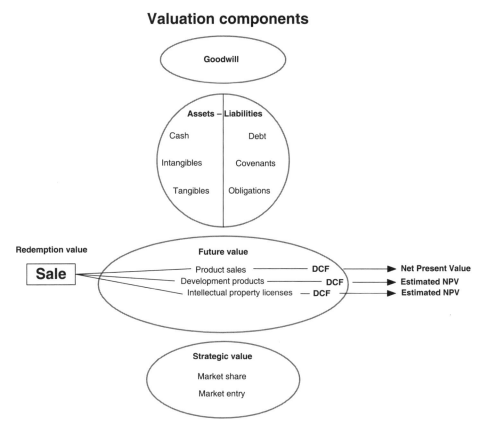

Figure 6.2 Valuation of an asset for sale

and this helps to reduce the cost which can be further improved where possible, by taking a licence in exchange for a one-time payment reducing the costs to the licensee and their assignees. Such a licence structure should also be as simple as possible and confer broad freedoms to use the process as required to develop and produce the product, and as noted above, it needs to contain the freedom to assign those rights as necessary to sub-licensees or acquirers of the product. Then, having established both the rights and freedoms to operate it will be possible to make an offer to out-license the product at full value. Similarly this process will be demanded by the licensee of such a product.

Deal structures

LICENCES

A licence is a permission from the owner of an asset to make use of the asset for specified purpose, period and in a defined geography. Other conditions may be applied within the licence but the key fact is that the ownership of the asset remains with the licensor even in the case where a licence has been granted which is exclusive, perpetual and irrevocable as may be the case with a technology integrated into a final product as it otherwise could not function without it.

The flexibility of a licence as opposed to ownership of an asset can be very broad. The terms of a licence may be written to suit the situation and can also vary over time as circumstances change. As already mentioned a licence may be exclusive between the two parties, permitting the licensee sole rights to the technology. Alternatively a non-exclusive licence can permit use of an asset which is a useful part of a product or even a complete product on a non-exclusive basis if this maximizes the return to the IP owner by increasing the competition for sales between several parties. As a result there is of course a premium to be paid for exclusivity and this is a major matter in many negotiations. A non-exclusive licence by contrast has lower value as it only gives freedom to operate rather than a competitive advantage as it confers no barrier to market entry over competitors. The choice between these two alternatives turns on whether the licensee requires protection and is willing to pay, or share, in the value that this brings. The selection therefore also becomes an integral part of the valuation of the opportunity and will be a fundamental assumption in the modelling of the product opportunity.

A licence's duration is for the most part specified to run to the end of the last patent protection available for the product and this may be defined at different levels such as active substance patents, method of use patents, patent extensions, formulation or other such protective mechanisms. Although these protections are highly regarded in the licensing of prescription medicines, licences for the use of brands are also highly sought after in the non-prescription (or OTC – over the counter) medicines business, as in this case the licence duration may be for a longer period. The protection of a brand name, and so the value this confers, does not expire with the patent, as is generally the case for a prescription-only medicine where the rapid availability of lower-priced generic versions of a product remove the incentive for investing in promotion. Perpetual licences are largely restricted to technologies with a low intrinsic value but which make up a part of the finished and more valuable product.

Exclusive licences may however be divided into geographic areas where a company which has a strong market presence but is restricted to a particular locality may be a good partner for a product. This is particularly so in specialty (typically hospital-based) medicines where a narrow prescriber base may mean that a company with a compatible portfolio and narrow focus can produce the best value from the product. In such a situation a series of exclusive licences may be granted to encompass the major markets of US, Europe and Japan as well as the emerging territories such as China and India where the recognition of foreign patents and licence rights through TRIPS and GATT are transforming the potential of those markets.

The price of a licence is therefore related to its ability to maintain a barrier to competitive entry to a market. Thus the terms for granting a licence will be structured to reflect not only the overall value of a product but the risk and timing of the realization of that value. In such circumstances one-time single licence payments for most pharmaceutical products would prove far too expensive and risky for the licensee. The risk of possible regulatory restrictions on the product's uses, the tractability of a market, the reimbursement hurdles and competitive environment can all have major negative effects on the sales potential of a product. As a result an upfront payment can either lose value for the licensor if it undervalues the asset or massively penalize the licensee if it underperforms. To counteract these risks staged payments using milestones and royalties are by far and away the best method of defraying the risk and ensuring an appropriate level of reward for the licensor. But this assumes that the licensor is able to withstand the deferment of their returns for many years. When estimating values it is worth remembering that while the development time for a product is in the order of 7 to 9 years before it reaches the market the time to reach peak sales can be as long again unless the marketing partner has the size to be able to mount simultaneous multi-country launches at a scale and power which can bring rapid market penetration. There are few companies which can mount this kind of effort with the consequence that most products will not see their aggregate peak until the patent life has all but expired, if they reach their potential peak sales target at all.

Royalty rates have become a battleground in recent years as the industry's dynamics have shifted more and more towards in-licensing of compounds to fuel growth. Private equity investment has created a supply of independently researched and developed products from the biotechnology (biotech) industry. Although the name has stuck the products of the companies in this 'biotech' sector may or may not be actually derived from biotechnological sources. In any case the financing that the products receive through the use of risk capital (venture capital) requires a greater return than was the case 20 to 30 years ago when compounds discovered in universities were developed by established pharmaceutical companies funded by large capital reserves (and so with a lower cost of capital). The use of risk capital has accelerated the demand for

returns and this is a major contributory factor to the pressure on negotiators in
all licensing transactions who have to seek seemingly ever-increasing payments
and royalties to provide a return to their investors. The old benchmarks for
royalty percentages are being redrawn to accommodate to this new factor (and
with regulatory hurdles also rising in an attempt to increase patient safety the
earnings growth of the bigger companies is becoming harder to achieve), yet
despite these increasing costs with the eventual dilution of earnings to preserve
competitive status a greater share of each product's earnings are being pledged to
smaller companies to secure the rights. This innovation premium will no doubt
find its correction point in time but with a 20-year base line for financial analysts
to define the result it is not likely that this trend will change in the near future.

A further possible division of a licence which has received attention is
the concept of splitting the therapeutic indications that a product can be used
to treat between different licensees. There will always be a debate about the
wisdom of this approach because of the potential for cross-use of the product
between disease indications and the requirement for consistent pricing. This
may undermine the justification for investing in additional clinical studies with
a consequent effect on the commercial value of such an approach. Even so, it
may be possible to differentiate the products by specialized formulations. This
can be a reasonable approach to generate more value from a product. However,
this differentiation of form to satisfy the requirements for a separate product
registration making it unlikely that one product form will be substituted easily
for another (as might be the case of an ampoule for injection compared to a
bottle of eye drops) is now frequently complicated by the attitude of national
reimbursement authorities. These authorities are becoming very intolerant
of pricing differentials for formulations of products based on an individual
molecule unless there is a very clear increase in the costs of producing one
formulation over another. As a result a licensee of a second indication may find
themselves tied to the price of the original product irrespective of their own
cost base. This can have serious implications for the profit margin of both forms
of the product and as a result the approach is questionable when considering
licence opportunities.

The flexibility this approach brings when applied to royalty rates means
that it is possible to institute a differential approach to rates depending upon
performance. Thresholds for performance can sit on either side of the product's
'true' sales forecast, allowing the provision for a step up in the royalty rate or
a step down according to the desired reward structure. In fact a series of steps
can be built into a tiered structure, which can give a steady improvement or a
tailing off, and these modifications can act as an incentive for a company to sell

more and so commit more resources. In the case of poor market performance, however, the licensor can be compensated by an increasing share of the smaller product sales value. These so-called 'collar' provisions may be applied only to each of the upside or downside conditions and they provide a mechanism to achieve equitability between the partners though the long and uncertain future of the product.

A further and useful financial mechanism within the licensing arena that gives additional scope for adjustments in compensation are sales-related milestone payments where, without altering the underlying royalty rate, a threshold of say $50 million in sales can be recognized and this may act as a top-up to a lower initial royalty rate and act as the signal to trigger a new rate to be used. This combination of deferrals, incentives and rewards means that licensing will remain the most frequently used transaction structure in the pharmaceutical industry as it recognizes the intrinsic risk and reward that is characteristic of the market.

A variation on the theme of licensing has emerged in the last 5 years where a combination of the features mentioned above are used by companies that have a broad portfolio of products but, for tactical reasons, need to concentrate their resources on only a few major products. In this situation the products which cannot receive adequate focus internally have been out-licensed to third-party companies for a fixed period in exchange for a share of their revenues. The arrangement permits the company to maintain the value of its asset and grant a licence limited to perhaps the period of 5 years, with the contracted right to recover the product. This can provide the means to assist the company on several fronts as the product sales can be consolidated into its balance sheet yet the company does not have to carry the overheads of a sales force and promotional costs beyond the fees included in the contract throughout the licence period during which the market share of the product is either defended or increased. This 'fostering' of the product may even be a useful precursor to a takeover of the marketing partner or, alternatively, if the licensing company's performance with its major products is sufficient, the fostered product might be sold to the fostering company to generate additional cash. The fostering and licence-back structure makes use of time limitation, exclusivity and performance enhancement features to ensure the healthy growth of a product. When considered in the context of portfolio management this means that the company can to some extent 'have its cake and eat it'. More will be said about creating and choosing such structural alternatives in the discussion of negotiation in Chapter 7, as each of the elements mentioned above has a bargaining value as well as an absolute value.

Alongside the issues of taking a licence for a product there are also opportunities to become a sublicensee for that product. In a master licence the right to sublicense is of great importance as this opens the opportunity to penetrate markets where a company does not have its own local presence. If the right to sublicense is not established in the initial contract the overall value of the products will be impaired. Depending on the status of the company taking the original licence the quality of the sublicensee may be critical, it is of note that many universities' technology transfer departments are becoming more sensitive to this consideration. In any case it is important to establish whether there are flow-through royalties to come to the originator in the case of a sublicence or whether the sublicence royalties accrue to the licensee alone. When constructing the licence the difference in value between these two situations must be factored into the price.

ACQUISITIONS

Acquisition should be considered in two major contexts: firstly the acquisition of products or other individual assets; secondly the acquisition of a company in total. This needs to be considered in a separate context because the risks and complexity of completing such transactions are significantly greater.

Acquiring products has a number of implications beyond those of taking a licence. When a company acquires a product it also acquires any and all liabilities already associated with that product. These liabilities may include past damages inflicted on patients, environmental impacts and contingent issues associated with third-party contracts. Conversely, the value represented in the acquisition of a product lies in obtaining the full value from its revenue streams and having full control of any development issues.

When making a product acquisition some of the major concerns are listed below:

- right and title
- licences
- manufacturing and technology transfer
- trademarks
- sublicensees
- continuing value
- covenants and change of control provisions.

It is a critical importance in undertaking an acquisition that the right and title of the vendor is established unequivocally. During the process of due diligence in the acquisition it is insufficient for the vendor to warrant ownership without severe penalties in the case of a mistake. Particularly in the area of biological agents, the massive increase in the number and complexity of patents filed to cover different parts of a biological process when compared to a small molecule product means that many patent litigation cases are now being brought against marketing companies with the intention of forcing a share of revenues from products which were previously believed to be unencumbered. An example of such a case where a so-called submarine patent (where the existence of the patent had not been notified to the market) occurred between Cambridge Antibody Technologies Ltd (CAT) and Abbott Laboratories and is indicative of the difficulties associated with biological products in general.

Abbott had taken a licence to CAT's antibody technology to create its product Humira for the treatment of rheumatoid arthritis, which was forecast to generate billions in sales. However, at the time of launching Humira, Abbott was notified by a small Australian biotech company called Peptech that Humira also required a licence to technology protected by Peptech's patents. As the value of Humira was now established Peptech not surprisingly held out for a significant royalty payment rate, much more than would have been granted earlier in the product's development when the risks were much higher. Abbott at first resisted the claims in court but eventually conceded that a licence was needed and negotiated this with Peptech. All of this would not have been of major note if Abbott had not also noticed that in their agreement with CAT that payment of any additional royalties surrounding the technology could be 'clawed back' or offset from the commitment to CAT. Abbott then proposed to enforce this. CAT naturally objected to this and subsequently after long litigation received a judgment which re-established their position. Although the claim and counter claims were ultimately resolved it was notable that there was a provision in CAT's accounts for the year when the case was being pursued for £7 million for legal costs. The company has now been acquired by AstraZeneca and the royalty streams sold on to a financial third party; still, this case gives an indication of the impact that submarine patents can have. If Abbott had for some reason divested Humira before all this occured, all the issues which they had to deal with would have become the responsibility of the acquiring company. This story emphasizes the need for extreme care in making acquisitions in general and in the biotechnology sector in particular. There is still much to be settled in law regarding biological patents which will only be resolved through the establishment of case law and this will only occur as cases are brought to the courts with all the expense that this entails.

Furthermore it is not just submarine patents on IP that can cause problems. There may also be issues relating to manufacture, obligations secured against product rights which may include leases, covenants for loan guarantees and similar structures which can lurk in a company behind a product as an unseen liability. In certain cases a product or other assets of a company may not even be divested without the permission of a financial institution or equity holder who holds such a covenant or lien. This can mean a requirement to make a settlement with that institution outside the terms of an acquisition and can add considerably to the costs of a transaction both in time and in money.

MANUFACTURING AND TRANSFER

Notwithstanding contractual issues there are practical considerations in the area of manufacturing which need to be taken into account as well. On a number of occasions I have come across the problem of the relocation of manufacturing as a requirement of a product acquisition. Where a product is being manufactured as a part of a multipurpose site, objections are frequently raised on the part of the group running the site that their capacity utilization will be affected so adversely as to make the site unprofitable. Although it is feasible to transfer manufacturing outside a company the impact of a transaction on the existing infrastructure can incur costs. These would need to be recovered from the acquirer and if they are too high could put them off. Such costs can usually be accounted for in the premium part of the product's valuation without necessarily signalling the cause. Manufacturing can also provide impediments to a transaction by having dedicated resources required for a process which cannot be shared with the acquirer. If this relates to hardware this would not ordinarily be a problem, but I was once involved in a situation requiring a technology transfer agreement where the reactor vessels required to make the product had to be of steel of sufficiently high quality to withstand the reagents used in the reactions. Because of this high quality the lead time to replicate them was 2 years. However, there was a corporate imperative to close the deal immediately. In the period before the new vessels could be produced and installed the existing manufacturing capacity would have to be used to serve two companies not one but, with two companies promoting the product the demand had doubled and so, as the vendor, we were required to ration supplies to our own company in order to satisfy the contract with the acquirer. Hence, remember that when assessing the costs and implications of an acquisition from either side of a deal the manufacturing issues deserve intimate attention as they can be can be very difficult to resolve.

TRADEMARKS

It is often the case that trademarks receive less attention than they deserve as I found many years ago when I was consulting to a firm in the animal health market. The firm had acquired an anthelminthic product for the treatment of worms in sheep, goats and camels. The product was principally sold to herders in the Middle East. The product range had been recently acquired and it was not until the new owner saw the sales figures for the first half year that they realized something was going drastically wrong. As a part of the acquisition plan the company had decided to update all the brand packaging to include their name and corporate trade dress; the salesmen had dutifully gone out with the newly packaged products during the dry season to oases on the migration trail, and in time-honoured fashion when the herders gathered at the marketplace each company's representative had stood up on a dais and held up their product for display to the customers who would come forward and buy each of the products they wanted. Needless to say the newly repackaged product received no recognition because the trademark (a picture of a camel) had gone. None of the herders had ever known the name of the product, which was written in English: they only bought the product because they knew the design on the packet, and without that the product had no market as it had lost its brand. The company in question had not bothered to acquire the trademarks as they had planned to change them and they were forced to go back and renegotiate rights to the trademarks, which obviously cost much more after the event, when the seller realized their value, than would have been the case if they had been included in the first place.

At a recent business development course I related this story and afterwards I was told by a physician that when he had started in a primary care practise in Germany he had been in a dispensing group and, when he made his first prescribing choices, as he did not know many products at that stage he would most often go for products from a manufacturer he knew to be good. As a consequence most of his patients were treated with the whole range of products from Merck & Co. as he had learned his pharmacology with the manual that they produced and which he kept at his bedside during revision. This just goes to show that whether the customer is a sophisticated Western physician or a simple herdsman the power of the trademark cannot be ignored.

SUBLICENSEES

In acquiring a product which has been marketed or co-developed there may be some licenses with persisting dependent rights to the product and so obligation to the sublicensees. Indeed some of these may be competitors at a global level yet become licensees on a regional basis through the acquisition of the product, a situation which may not be compatible with your own policies. Careful study of these licence agreements is required to understand whether or not you may terminate these agreements post-acquisition and under what terms. If nothing exists in the contract the only alternative may be to offer to buy out such agreements. This may require considerable time in negotiations as you will probably have an unwilling counterparty to deal with. There will be some significant rights within contracts of this kind, such as a lengthy cancellation period, which can cause considerable disruption to global plans such as a rebranding programme.

CHANGE OF CONTROL

A change of control provision in a contract states that if the ownership of a product or the licensor of a product is acquired by a third party that the licensee or other contracted party may have the right to renegotiate or terminate the contract. If the value of the product rests on their provision of services this may have significant implications for the value of the asset. Moreover change of control provisions in a contract may be fully specified or, depending on the language used, may be implied and in either case this requires that the acquisition process is managed with extreme care to preserve the value in the product. The issue of change of control relates not only to certain licensees and their rights but through them to the overall continuing value of the asset itself. When an asset changes hands it is not only the sublicensees who have a say: wholesalers, distributors, agents and representatives may each take the opportunity to try and revise and improve the terms of their relationship with your company through their contract. Another transaction in which I was involved required the transfer of a product from one company to another which included a dedicated sales force in the US whose employment, on paper at least, was to be transferred with the product to the new owner. However, at the same time as we were trying to execute this transaction many of the major companies in the US had started recruitment drives and were paying tens of thousands of dollars in signing-on bonuses for experienced representatives. As soon as the field force we wanted to transfer found that their employer was to change many took the opportunity to jump ship. Our challenge was to maintain the value of the asset and to do this we had to continually replace these experienced representatives to maintain the field coverage of the hospitals and so the sales. Wherever possible we matched the signing-on bonuses by paying retaining bonuses rather than be left with nothing but the new recruits which was a very costly exercise. Simultaneously the management of the contract field force which had been operating alongside the in-house representative decided to try and renegotiate their terms which further compounded the problem. Changes of control are most definitely best dealt with when setting up a contract rather than fixing when the deal is in full swing.

The future value of a product which is the subject of a licence has a different character when compared to the method for valuing a product for sale. A vendor will need to add a premium to the underlying cash flows as the total value of the product is being transferred not just the sales line or profit contribution and this is likely to have a persisting value beyond a reasonable forecast period. The market at present has seen a steady increase in prices paid for products at acquisition as a very active market has emerged in re-profiling and relaunching products. Older products which have a lengthy sales history have usually been valued on a multiple of sales using a discounted cash flow model. The multiple chosen depends on the slope of the sales curve and may vary between one times the last year's sales up to six times that amount if the product is still growing. In addition it is common practice to attach a 'terminal value' to the multiple to make up the total purchase price. In a discounted cash flow valuation, the cash flow is projected for each year into the future for a number of years (usually five – after that time individual annual cash flows cannot be forecast with any reasonable accuracy). At that point, rather than attempting to forecast the cash flow for each individual year, a single value is used to represent the discounted value of the subsequent cash flows before a multiple of the last forecast year's sales – often between two- to three-fold is calculated. This single value is called the 'terminal value'.

The terminal value of a marketed product may represent a reasonable proportion of the overall valuation. This is in contrast to the terminal value of a piece of manufacturing equipment at the end of its useful life, which is usually taken to be its salvage value, often less than 10 per cent of the current value. By contrast, the terminal value associated with a product whose sales are not in steep decline may be more than 50 per cent of the total present value. For this reason, the terminal value calculation is often highly debated when performing such a valuation. When using this valuation technique, however, the fundamental issue is the strength of the forecast of sales which itself will depend on the robustness of the market model. The final figure asked for a product which is to be acquired may therefore be relatively high and so may not attract many bidders, which is a requirement for achieving good value in a sale.

As most large companies are continuously faced with the need to manage their portfolios of products to improve the average maturity and so corporate growth, they are usually seeking ways to divest themselves of older products.

One way of modifying the hurdle of the price for such a product which, being older will be less attractive to strong, well-funded companies and more attractive to smaller but less well-funded firms, is to change the basis of payment for the product. The ability of smaller companies to do a 'take-out' purchase for cash will quite often be severely restricted by a lack of funds and the ability to borrow the large amounts required. Consequently a more typical route is to use an 'earn-out' formula (see Figure 6.3) by which, after making a down-payment, the acquiring company will each year return a share of the profits on a depreciating basis until they have discharged the cost of the acquisition. In this way the acquiring company can use the asset as the means to leverage its own purchase. Naturally the vendor must satisfy themselves that the acquirer has the ability to achieve their projected sales figures and this can, on occasion, lead them to accept a lower offer from a 'safer' bidder in preference to a more ambitious bid from a less substantial company. This part of the valuation equation will rely upon rigorous due diligence by the vendor rather than that of the acquirer.

As mentioned above the market for these products has become very active through the advent of many 'specialty pharma' companies in the last 10 years and this has meant that product assets are now rarely made available without an auction process which in itself can be a challenging undertaking.

SPECIFIC DUE DILIGENCE ISSUES

The issues which may be encountered in the due diligence process during product acquisitions can be many and varied. Probably the most frequently

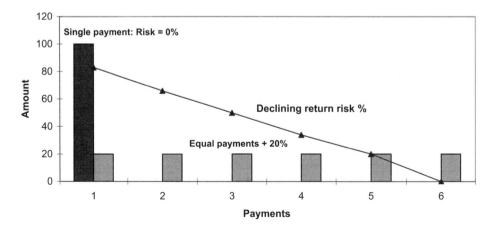

Figure 6.3 Take-out versus earn-out value

encountered is poor documentation and this is the source of some of the gravest errors. As products become older and of less importance to a company, the rigour with which documentation is pursued falls off dramatically and understandably this is not an area which attracts much investment or attention. As a result, when trying to research the issues of contract liabilities, patent maintenance, manufacturing batch records and customer sales records, the lack of documentation can be daunting but persistence and patience will enable you to avoid inheriting liabilities with the product.

Another issue which can impair a purchase is the maintenance of inventory. While finished product inventory is paramount it is no less important to attend to supply chain components and materials. Particularly when a product has been scheduled for divestment, production managers will become hesitant to place future orders for components for fear of building up inventory that will have to be written off. Once there is a reduction in order frequency or size the component manufacturers on noting this will reduce their own inventories accordingly which may continue until people are waiting for orders before starting a batch run with the result that the whole chain slows and becomes unstable. This can lead to a hiccup in supplies of say active produce ingredients (APIs) reaching the factory and so disruption of the supply chain. Control of the information regarding a product sale from business development is therefore important for managing this aspect of product value. When acquiring a product it is just as necessary to ensure that the supply chain of the target product is intact all the way back to basic materials. This is also true of trade dressed materials as once the product has changed hands any existing stock in its old packaging may need to be re-dressed and even repackaged which will have a bearing on costs. One temporary solution can be to over-sticker existing stock but regulatory authorities are reluctant to permit this continuing for too long.

If any special machinery is to be transferred with the product then a specialist must check the age, state of repair and mobility of this equipment and that the final delivery facility has the capacity to contain it. During one acquisition, the head of manufacturing was only just in time in noticing that the incoming machines were actually half a metre taller than the headroom in the facility where they were due to be delivered and as a result the manufacturing had to be re-sited, and this brought unbudgeted costs.

It is not just machines which have surprises in store. During the due diligence for a financial investment we found that one of the portfolio companies had made an acquisition in which the formulation process was to be transferred from the US to a European facility. Whilst the transfer was quickly achieved unfortunately the process could not be made to produce product which would pass quality control despite following the standard operating procedures laid down to the letter. It was only when we interviewed a retired member of staff from the acquired company that we found that an additional step had been introduced without documentation and that if it were not performed the product formulation would separate after mixing. The know-how for such an operation is not necessarily contained within a due diligence data room. Site visits and interviews with manufacturing staff are strongly recommended in these circumstances.

Another component of the product acquisition is the goodwill that goes with the brand. I discussed this above in the example of the camel worm powder. That story, while it points out the pitfalls of overlooking such attributes, also supports the notion that goodwill, although intangible, has real value. However, goodwill quite often also represents the intangible premium desired by the owners of the selling company. In order to ascertain the 'true' value of this goodwill rather than the opinion of the perceived and sometimes egotistically motivated value of the owners, it is worth interviewing customers to find out whether there is any real goodwill or whether this can be a bargaining point in the negotiation of the price of the acquisition.

At closing it is necessary to ensure that the transaction is completed in total, or 'perfected' as it is sometimes called. This requires that there is a comprehensive exchange of documents and an overseeing of certain specific activities. The first of these is the re-registration of the marketing authorizations, manufacturing licences and pharmaco-vigilance activities. Secondly an audit of the inventory management process is carried out and, where necessary, contracts and representation are secured in all territories. As a part of this process it is advisable to set up an escrow account held by a third party such as a bank to compensate the vendor in the case of any default on the part of the acquirer or sometimes vice versa. Performance criteria can be set for closing, inventory control, technology transfer and the provision of know-how. If the product has been sold on an earn-out basis there should also be a penalty for underperformance in the marketplace. The escrow account ensures that funds are available for compensation according to contracted formulae and avoid disputes of interpretation post-closure.

COMPANY ACQUISITIONS

Company acquisitions differ from product acquisitions in the complexity of the transaction and the separate and overlying complications associated with equity ownership which itself is usually divided amongst many shareholders with different motivations. A primary consideration in considering a company acquisition is whether the company is publicly traded or privately held. In either case as discussions progress it is necessary to recognize that shareholders have rights to information from their management. In the past there have been a number of instances where company managements have entertained bids from potential acquirers without informing more than a few of the shareholder base and the demands of good corporate governance require equal disclosure. Hence even as the potential acquirer it is necessary to ensure that the counterparty is following the rules on their side to protect the possible deal. In an increasingly litigious market and with corporate governance requiring transparency at all levels the responsibility for disclosure goes equally for both sides of the table. In consequence and in particular among the larger companies there is a constant potential for conflict between the interests of boards with the responsibility to maximize shareholder value and the shareholders themselves who will have many different views on what constitutes value at any given time.

When considering an acquisition of a publicly traded company it is necessary to understand the listing rules of the markets on which they trade. These rules may not be familiar to individuals and so local advice should be sought to establish whether each market has different rules and what consequences these may have for a given transaction. It is also worth remembering that delisting threshold requirements, that is what percentage of total shares must be controlled by the acquiring company may also vary between markets. In Germany for instance the threshold has required that greater than 90 per cent ownership of shares be controlled before the target company can be de-listed from its existing exchange. This has compared unfavourably with London where a threshold of 70 per cent has been more common. There is another a threshold which affects the level of ownership required to be able to force a 'squeeze-out' of minority shareholders to obtain 100 per cent ownership of a company which can be as high as 75 per cent before a tender offer must be accepted by the minority shareholders.

There are many options for financing company acquisitions. The simplest may be to utilize retained earnings in the company but this should be compared with borrowing or 'leverage' as it is called as the costs of borrowing can have less impact on the company if it maintains its financial reserves and services the debt from revenue. This is an attractive option for companies with steady growth in earnings in excess of the amount needed to service debts. The major alternative to a cash purchase is to offer stock either directly to the shareholders of the target company, possibly with warrants or options to secure their value (the act as a guarantee of value), or to make a 'secondary offering' of new shares to the capital markets to raise more cash without borrowing. There are a huge number of variations on these two basic models which suit different companies at different times and these are chosen based on their relative risks and costs.

Another chance to finance an acquisition may lie in the utilization of assets within either of the companies which will not be required in the merged company. These assets may either be sold or potentially spun out as a new company and floated by initial public offering (IPO) to provide the funds, or, alternatively, it might first be funded by private equity. Moreover the opportunity to use an earn-out structure for a management buy-out (an MBO) which, as in the product acquisition, can defer the economics of the transaction for the acquirers might be considered as might the use of a special purpose vehicle (SPV) to act as a temporary and virtual company to develop assets. Although use of SPVs became questionable due to certain abuses some years ago these structures can still be put to good use if the governance is transparent. In addition to these options a reverse merger into a 'shell' company is a possibility. These come about because in such a high risk market there are always situations where companies have achieved significant funding for promising scientific ideas, yet the research has failed. These companies become the target of reverse mergers when technology rich suitor companies with little cash go seeking a compatible partner who has cash but due to the research failure no products. The resulting merger can create value where before there was none.

Sources of finance for company acquisitions as mentioned above can be from reserves or maybe taken a senior or subordinated debt. Alternatively a bond may be issued with various characteristics offering an annuity, a balloon payment or a combination of the two. A variety of convertible structures have been utilized for this purpose as asset sales and the use of the target's balance sheet. There has also been a place for royalty transactions where the future-value of product cash flows are securitized to provide capital in the near term to achieve a company acquisition.

When considering equity transactions some of the most significant issues to be considered are the valuation of the shares offered at the time of the offer and then at that date of closing which can vary, sometimes quite widely. Another factor which can have a bearing on the attraction of an equity transaction are the requirements for 'lock-up' periods where shares cannot be traded for a defined time following the closing of the transaction. This can be a serious concern to private equity holders as there is an unknowable quantity of risk implied by waiting for the lock-up period to end and this will induce a very cautious approach to valuation as a result. Furthermore the ownership structure of a company can lead to a number of additional negotiations if the share classes owned by different shareholders have different rights from each other. There may be preference rights associated with certain classes of share and these may include independent negotiating rights in the case of an acquisition. It can also be the case that warrants to buy shares and granted options may have a right to respectively be exercised or vest in the case of acquisition and that this can affect the intrinsic valuation of the company unless and until these interests are satisfied.

On a more general level, when considering the due diligence matters involved in a company acquisition it is always advisable to take counsel from local lawyers in the case of trans-national transactions. Reasons for this include the fact that many European countries still have different waiting periods for transaction closings to occur and different regulations requiring publications and notifications of a change of ownership. Each of these can invalidate a transaction and if they are not completed in a timely fashion and the asset may become impaired due to disruptions in supply or representation. Trades unions in some countries can exercise considerable rights on behalf of the employees and can block or modify arrangements negotiated between companies and their owners if they feel that their members are being disadvantaged. They may also delay the closure of a transaction if this might prove to be a bargaining tool for pay and conditions after the merger. If it is the case that staff will be made redundant the obligations of the employer need to be well understood. In France for instance it is still the case that the social contract requires that a person being made redundant must have their social security contributions paid up until their retirement date by the employer if the redundancy is forced. In the past several US companies have found this information out too late to prevent having provided a pension for many 30-year-olds. A newly empowered issue of major significance to acquisitions are the environmental obligations which become the responsibility of the acquiring company. An environmental impact study of the company's current activities should be undertaken in every case as a matter of urgency. Strict liability for retrospective environmental damage is coming into force throughout Europe and the US is soon to follow suit. The costs of land remediation, water remediation and consequential damages have yet to be estimated in a pharmaceutical context but if the example provided by the liability claims for adverse clinical events is followed the amounts involved could be very high indeed.

When acquiring assets outside of Europe and the US it is also an absolute requirement to establish that the land the site stands in is in the ownership of the company. There have been several instances where foreign acquisitions have been made only to find that the asset is in fact leased and not owned.

In many other instances all over Europe and the Far East at the current time companies are also receiving funds from regional grants, loans which are secured against covenants to remain in one location for a number of years and other similar constraints designed to protect local investment. When conducting due diligence in these circumstances it is always necessary to look for these potential problems.

Closing a company acquisition takes a considerable effort in human resources, time and legal fees. In order that this work is successful or at least protected from failure a remedial mechanism needs to be put in place to deal with issues which arise after the closing has occurred. These may be in the form of contracts as in the right to make clawbacks in the case that a warranty or representation was unfounded. This may lead to the imposition of penalties to be taken from an escrow account if the assets have proved not to have the represented worth. As always in closing a transaction it is an absolute requirement to ensure that all assignments and registrations necessary for the perfection of the transaction are undertaken.

Other deal structures

Among the other deals structures which are available are joint ventures, distribution agreements, agency agreements, option agreements and special purpose vehicles. Both distribution and agency agreements are in effect special kinds of licence but they lack the commitment from the licensor to maintain their relationship in the event that performance of the deal criteria are not met. The relationship in an agency agreement is stronger than that for a distributor and, as the name suggests, the agent actively promotes the product in exchange for a proportion of the sales revenue. In most distribution agreements the relationship is not as close as the distributor takes less of an active part in the promotion of the product. Distributors will typically include the product in a catalogue carried on behalf of a number of clients. Both relationships, however, require the distributor or agent to carry a minimum level of stock, to meet minimum sales criteria and to maintain customer records. The main difference between these types of agreements and a full licence is that distribution agreements are easily severable, often merely by notifying the distributor and waiting for the notice period stipulated in the contract to expire. Agency agreements being closer contain many more protections for the agent in the event of underperformance. The agent also will have incentives and a direct relationship with the marketing group of the principal. In other respects the rights and duties of the two parties in either agreement structure can be similar to those under a licence.

JOINT VENTURES

Joint ventures may be initiated for a variety of purposes and in the pharmaceutical industry one of the more common reasons for a joint venture is a research collaboration. This then begins to generate novel intellectual property which can become the object of a potentially valuable commercial venture. However, the reason for forming a joint venture is that there is a dependency between the two parties by the sharing of skills, expertise or resources which neither has alone. The sharing of the costs and risks can make sense in such a speculative venture. Yet there are complications in such an arrangement which need to be considered before proposing a joint venture.

One of the most contentious of these issues is: who has control? Many joint ventures are started on the basis of a 50:50 ownership and because of this later run into problems if the owners disagree about the future direction of the venture. This can lead to the dissolution of the venture with one party buying out the other – which can itself become a complex transaction. In other situations joint ventures have been made where one partner has a dominating share a 51:49 relationship. I was involved in one of these during the 1980s. Unfortunate disagreements at board level frequently spilled into the operating business making commercial success difficult to achieve. It was only when the 51 per cent partner seized control and insisted on the company being operated as a subsidiary that some kind of order was restored. Even then the constraints of operating with such a spilt at the top meant that, after a few years, as the venture was situated in the territory of the 49 per cent partner, it was sold back to them and a separate subsidiary started by the 51 per cent partner.

On a commercial basis therefore joint ventures can be extraordinarily difficult to manage without a complete accord between the partners. Even a successful joint venture such as the AstraMerck joint venture created for the launch and promotion of Prilosec (omeprezole) in the US (which created a brand leader) had major consequences at the programmed end of the agreement: the break-up costs were a reported $3.3 billion in a compensation package to Merck, which came at a difficult time for AstraZeneca. All joint ventures therefore are fraught with problems and need very careful consideration before selecting this as the preferred structure compared to the many others available.

Another structure which has come into vogue in the last few years is the granting or taking of an option to a development-level product. The concept behind such an option is the provision of a fixed level of cash which secures the product for the partner but does not obligate it to either take the product or fund it further. Yet having this option prevents the product falling into the hands of a competitor if it proves to be of high worth as its development programme unfolds. Genentech granted options to Roche on its pipeline of products: as each product finishes its proof of concept studies Roche may exercise its option to license the products on a first refusal basis. Similarly Novartis paid $50 million to Idenix for an option to license a Phase II compound, and a smaller amount to Morphosys for options to pipeline products in the recent past. There are advantages to both parties because of the lack of commitment and the provision of funds; however, if the option is not exercised by the partnering company this may adversely affect the future worth as it may raise questions about the motive of the partner in abandoning a significant investment, even if the grounds for doing so were of a purely commercial nature.

SPECIAL PURPOSE VEHICLES

A special purpose vehicle (SPV) uses a separate legal entity to aggregate the assets, money and people required to perform a specific project. The advantage of this kind of structure is that people working for the vehicle need not be located in any specific place nor even do they need to have their employment contracts assigned to the vehicle. This may avoid costly infrastructure changes and pension scheme disruptions yet reassigns the newly created assets to new ownership. It can be particularly useful where a team whom a company wishes to retain for future projects might otherwise have to be redeployed or released. The objective of such an SPV can be to develop a specific product or portfolio without the disruption of setting up a wholly new company. The project or products in the SPV may be bought or sold independently from the main company as it is the vehicle which owns the IP contained within it. Furthermore the vehicle may be sold in total, or might be floated independently on a stock exchange to become a new and separate company. At the inception funding can be provided by private investors or banks without affecting the equity holdings of the parent company or its degree of leverage, leaving its role as an investor in-kind through the contribution of its IP. When the venture is sold or the products are acquired, maybe by the original parent company, the value created is released to the investors. Figure 6.4 indicates the general structure of such a vehicle.

It is worth noting that along with the risk the control of the development must be passed to the SPV's management. The transparency this affords ensures that the legal issues affecting some past SPVs which caused problems though inappropriate governance can be overcome.

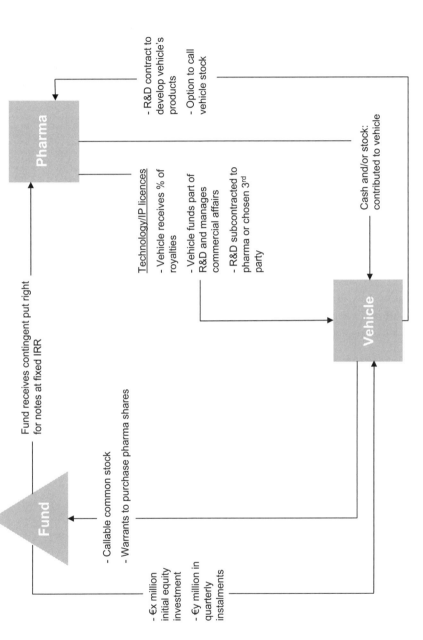

Figure 6.4 Special purpose vehicle

In considering which of these structures suits your company best is important to consider the following issues:

- resource comparison

- portfolio fit

- financial strength

- management depth

- dependence on success.

The balance between these issues will determine which structure fits the company, both now and in the future. As a company grows it will be able to enter into agreements utilizing a number of different structures. Therefore its management needs to have the skills and information to choose and use the best structures to complement their existing situation. As a result monitoring of the use of resources, the fit with a company's existing portfolio including its own and its in-licensed products, the network of relationships the company can manage and the degree and a balance of risk across that portfolio need to be continuously maintained and updated and these tasks sit well within the remit of a business development function.

Due Diligence and Negotiations

Due diligence

Before it is possible to enter full negotiations with a company or institution for the rights to a product or technology it is necessary to establish that the claims made for that asset are both true in the sense of being represented honestly and that the scientific basis and regulatory requirements have been satisfied appropriately. Moreover it is necessary to establish that the company has right and title to the asset without encumbrances. The process by which this is done is generally referred to as 'due diligence'.

In preparing for due diligence both sides of the transaction need to collect and collate the information which will be required by the counterparty to establish all the various points needed to close the transaction. The general categories of information required relate to items under the headings:

- intellectual property
- contractual relations
- human resources
- ownership structure
- operational liabilities and assets
- business plan.

Each of these items will have a variety of aspects suited to the individual case so, for instance, IP relates to patents owned by the company or university and any third-party patents that have had to be licensed, which the new IP depends upon for freedom to operate. A list of the items which one would expect to provide or receive during a due diligence process for owned patents might be:

- patent numbers

- summary of claims

- relationship between claims

- issue dates, expiry dates, potential supplementary protections

- oppositions and challenges (previous and existing)

- a schedule of extensions to be filed.

For licensed-in patents the list would also be:

- licensed-in contracts

- patent numbers

- summary of claims

- relation between claims

- issue dates, expiry dates, potential supplementary protections

- oppositions and challenges (previous and existing)

- a schedule of extensions to be filed.

In establishing a due diligence process it is quite usual to create a 'data room' where copies of all the relevant documents are stored in an archive which is referenced just as in a library for easy access. The data room should be isolated and preferably equipped with desks for the visiting due diligence team to be seated so that they can use the data room like the reading room of a library. The process of giving and receiving data in a project is streamlined by having a symmetrical understanding between the parties and this is best achieved by the exchange of a due diligence requirements list prior to a physical visit. In this way any outstanding matters can be researched and appropriate data located by the providing party beforehand. On the topic of contractual relationships these might relate to:

- distributors

- licensing-out

- licensing-in

- academic collaborations

- non-government organizations

- agents

- supply and manufacturing

- clinical research organizations

- settlements.

And these should contain details of the costs and revenues related to each contract.

Furthermore, for each contract it will be necessary to have a record of:

- the name of the counterparty

- the type of contract

- jurisdiction (that is country law)

- contract end date

- summary of key issues

- change of control consequences

- effect of competition and exclusivity

- and a full copy of the contract and any codicils or addenda.

In particular where concerning a company acquisition the human resources description should contain:

- an organization chart

- a list of the personnel including their:
  - function and role
  - entry date
  - remuneration schedule

- contracts for key personnel

- special issues such as staff with important knowledge which could reduce the value of the company if they are not retained.

Additionally, in the instance of a company acquisition, the ownership structure should be explained including the:

- capitalization table

- share classes if any

- subsidiaries

- shareholders' agreement

- covenants.

It may be that due to the sensitivity of personal data and market-sensitive data some of these items should be held separately from the data room under the control of the legal department and available only to qualified individuals in the counterparty's team, even when a confidentiality agreement is in place. Although the due diligence team will be constrained to silence issues such as remuneration can stimulate comments which can be unhelpful later in a partnership.

The operational liabilities and assets of the company should include all contractual, legal and financial commitments both on and off the balance sheet such as:

- bank loans

- bank guarantees

- escrow accounts

- leases.

It should also include a list of all assets including:

- financial assets (shares and other financial instruments)

- tangible assets

- intangible assets (brands, trademarks and so on).

Depending on the circumstances the business plan for a product or for a company in total should be provided including but not limited to:

- sales histories

- sales forecasts

- inventory accounts

- profit and loss (by product)

- clinical development plans

- competition analysis

- contingent issues such as manufacturing, supply chain

- market models and forecasts.

The due diligence process therefore requires the exchange of the detailed lists that are appropriate to the particular transaction and then the construction of teams on both sides which can both ask the relevant questions from their own speciality and receive the answers from the appropriate source on the other side. Such a team may include representatives from research, manufacturing, finance, marketing and clinical development as well as the business development operatives. The business development function should lead the team and have authority over the other functions as business development will be in charge of maintaining coherence during the transaction process. As such the team should be briefed by business development on the strategic issues which have been authorized by senior management in the company. These will include the degree of engagement and the commitment of the company to completing the transaction, and its relative worth. As a consequence the team selection needs to be made by business development, who should choose people from each speciality with the correct and sufficient experience to undertake the task. It may sometimes also be useful for a speciality to 'double team' in order for newer members of that speciality to gain experience in performing due diligence under the guidance of a more senior and experienced person before operating alone later.

Of crucial importance is that during the process of due diligence only one 'face and voice' is presented to the counterparty, there is always a risk that during the due diligence process individuals engage in conversations on a one-to-one basis which are then not shared with the remainder of the team. It is mandatory that all communications are noted during due diligence and reported back to the other members of the team throughout the process. It is the responsibility of the business development leader to ensure that all required information is logged, recorded and communicated.

The due diligence process may be conducted in several parts; indeed, it may take place over a number of months and at several different locations. Consequently, collation of the knowledge gathered into an aggregate report which can become part of the archive of the transaction is of the highest importance. As indicated above the structure of this report can be structured on the on-going checklist of items of information which will be required in order to complete the transaction. It is also quite likely that the due diligence process cannot be completed merely between the two parties themselves. Third-party validation through market research, expert opinion and other professional bodies such as accountants, auditors, credit agencies and others may be required. The purpose of this due diligence is to protect the company's interest from the consequences of an incomplete or imperfect transaction. There are multiple examples of companies having finished transactions only to find that the asset they have acquired or licensed is impaired by unforeseen liabilities, issues with manufacturers or other commercial limitations which would have been exposed if the due diligence performed had been broadly based rather than overly concentrated on scientific issues alone.

Structuring due diligence into different phases will be useful. They might include initial due diligence, which establishes the key issues for the transaction. Incidental, trivial or standard issues can be left as they can be checked in detail later and only when the parties have committed to the transaction. This spares the costs of engaging external counsel or financial advisors for opinions and validations until it is sure that the investment in their time will be worthwhile. It is therefore useful on each occasion to decide what are likely to be the critical issues for the specific transaction and to ensure that these are dealt with early in the process.

As the due diligence progresses the team should be brought together regularly and debriefed by the business development leader. At this meeting a list of items which are either unresolved or unsatisfactory should be made, building up a list of issues which need to be included in the term sheet and will later be proposed to the counterparty as a part of the negotiation process. If there are impairments, uncertainties or liabilities which are not 'show-stoppers' or 'deal breakers' these can be factored into the term sheet either by a reduction in the valuation, or perhaps as a contingent offset to the cost which can be applied to the valuation of the asset if it becomes relevant. In the same way any other sort of liability may be treated on a contingency basis. If an event may not occur or if the outcome is not acceptable this possibility can be foreseen in the contract and the contingent actions stipulated.

The due diligence process provides an inventory of facts around which the negotiation can be conducted. In setting out these facts there is a great similarity between the creation of a contract and the creation of a computer program. In a computer program the subroutines are constructed from a series of declarations which then become the variables against which the operators are applied. The typical structure of 'if, then, else' operators found in a computer program using a language like Basic, can deal with even complex relationships between facts. Due diligence establishes both the existence of a fact which appears in the contract as declaration and its value and relationship to other facts and events for the purposes of the contract can be stated.

Above all, full documentation of due diligence undertaken for a transaction will be the basis for both the creation of the contract and an audit of its performance. As a consequence it builds up a body of knowledge which constitutes an image of the value of the product. This also forms the substance of the negotiation of the terms and conditions and ultimately the final price of the transaction to be agreed and settled by both parties.

Negotiations

The subject of negotiations involves discussion of techniques including social psychology, games theory and personality. It has been said that almost every interaction between people has some elements of a negotiation, this may be something of an exaggeration but when people are involved in a formal negotiation they quite often overlook their existing everyday negotiating skills or the lack of them. When undertaking a negotiation on behalf of a company it is the responsibility of the individuals to ensure that their practices are of the best standard. This involves some understanding of negotiation theory but more importantly negotiation practice. For many people in the pharmaceutical industry because negotiations are largely performed in English they may also be negotiating in a second language. This can lead to perfectly honest misunderstandings through inappropriate use or comprehension of the language which requires continuous and thorough review of all agreements and undertakings made during a negotiation by a qualified person with an excellent command of the language in use. As is so frequently the case in business development this requires accurate recording of the information exchanged in order that, as much as possible, miscommunications are resolved or avoided at the earliest possible stage. It can be very costly to have to return to a negotiated point later in a transaction because of a misunderstanding as all subsequent points may rest on this one and then require redrafting of the agreement. Hence a clear negotiating plan is of great assistance at each stage of the negotiation to ensure that all points are covered during each discussion and the resolution of points which were not be addressed in the last session is not forgotten. In this situation mind mapping is a very useful tool as it permits a wide variety of points to be collected from the team and collates them into a document (see Figure 7.1). Each team member can use this document to keep track of proceedings and then make their own contributions.

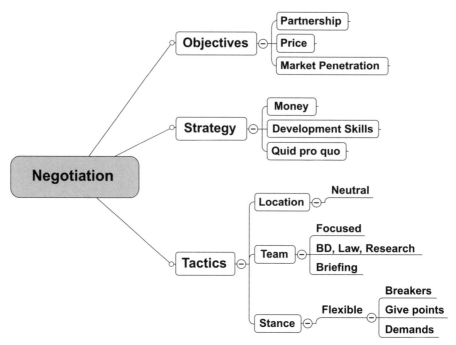

Figure 7.1   Negotiation mind map

NEGOTIATION PLAN

The negotiation plan can refer once more to the basic building blocks of transaction building – Objectives, Strategy and Tactics. In each negotiation, whether it is the whole deal or a stepping-stone meeting on the way, a clear objective should be set. This might be to achieve clarity on a particular point, to establish the principal rights and duties of the parties or, a value range for the transaction. If the objective is clear to the team before going in then the strategy and roles used to achieve it can be planned. I was once invited to join a negotiating team by the general manager of a company. He wanted to persuade his medical director to make the commitment to back a specific project rather than pursue a broader plan which the medical director felt was less risky but the general manager felt lacked commitment and would cost more as well as take too long. He asked me to attend the meeting with him and yet to say nothing until he addressed me, at which point I should choose an appropriate phrase to agree with what he'd asked. As the discussion unfolded he manoeuvred the medical director to the point of the decision. The general manager then turned to me and said, 'From the marketing perspective will we succeed if we do this?' to which I replied, 'Of course!' The extra pressure of the 'independent' witness persuaded the, still somewhat doubtful, medical director to make the commitment – the plan had worked perfectly!

One fundamental point to be considered though is the nature of the negotiation. In political and particularly military circumstances a negotiation is the peaceful alternative to conflict. As a result negotiations are very often portrayed as having a win or lose outcome. As has been pointed out by many courses and books on the subject, in commercial circumstances the objective should more properly be win–win, if the purpose is to strike a bargain which is acceptable to both sides. If not – why enter the negotiation? There are, however, from experience rather too many people in the industry who measure their success by how much of a penalty their counterparty has to accept before the deal can be done. I have observed a tendency to abuse a powerful position particularly among people representing bigger companies. Although I'm not suggesting that 'big pharma' should act with humility I hold the view that a more powerful party to a negotiation has the responsibility to act with suitable respect for their counterparty. Unfortunately in many cases the attitude of representatives of smaller companies tends to reinforce the imbalance.

By way of example: in business development courses, I have run simulated negotiation, on several occasions where two teams are invited to strike a deal by acting as the negotiators for two companies based on the profiles of a development-level company with an interesting new product and an established company with a marketed product. Each time the simulation has been run, despite each of the teams of 'players' coming from a mixture of both small and large companies, the characterization given to the marketed product company is aggressive and exploitative while the development-level company is portrayed by the role players as the supplicant and in a weak position. Even when the teams are briefed to play the contrary roles the 'dominance' and 'weakness' creeps back into the exchanges until each has taken up an antagonistic position where the bigger company sets out to abuse the smaller by taking advantage of their strength.

This observation from a teaching situation is borne out in real negotiations where I advise clients who are approaching big companies with a product opportunity. My own time in big pharma companies provided many examples of individuals, within my own company and in other large firms who knowingly or not 'took on the mantle' of the size of their company to act out a dominating role, but ended up feeding their ego rather than serving the needs of the company. In setting out the negotiation plan therefore it is necessary to take a view of the respective sizes of the companies and their motivation for entering discussions. If a company is seeking to auction an asset of high value which is sought after by many large companies a very different attitude is required in the negotiation to that required if the company is seeking its first and validating partnership for a new technology – a situation where all the power lies on one side of the table. The real purpose of the negotiation is to reach an agreement and the main point of difference is likely to be on the valuation. As seen above, because this is subjective there will often be a gap between the expectations between the two sides.

One phrase that is frequently used to try and obtain the right balance between the parties is 'in good faith' or in Latin *bona fides*. This implies that there aside from its strict legal interpretation there will be an attempt made to reach an equitable solution by both sides. Good faith is the embodiment of the essence of a contract requiring both parties to work together, hence to negotiate in good faith implies that this is the desired outcome.

The negotiation plan therefore needs to set out the objective for the company and to recognize the opportunities and constraints that both your own side and the counterparty have to work with to seek the best way forward.

What then might be the elements of such a plan? In the case of a licensing deal it might be to secure the worldwide development and marketing rights to a product from an originating company. That's fine but is insufficient as a description of the transaction outcome that your company might desire. Certain other criteria will also need to be met to satisfy the objective according to the situation. Will the rights be exclusive? What about manufacturing rights? Co-promotion rights? Continued development of the compound for other indications? All such criteria need to be laid out and agreed internally before engaging with the negotiating partner. This may be conducted as a debate amongst peers or decided unilaterally by senior management, after consultation with internal constituencies in the company and once their relative levels of importance have been gauged. These criteria are supplementary to the product profile achieved earlier as they affect the way that the product can be brought into the market through the use of internal resources and so affect the ability to convert the potential of the product into value. But they are also vital components in the negotiation process as they may be traded one against another to mould the agreement into a workable contract between the parties. Thus the negotiation plan also becomes an inventory of bargaining chips, absolute requirements, desirable additions and issues to be avoided.

As a result this inventory will provide the basis for an assessment of the right personnel to understand, articulate and communicate the company's needs to the counterparty. This team should also be matched to the team they are going to meet on the other side of the table. The strategy of taking the correct resources into a negotiation is paralleled by military planning techniques which select the right number of people for a task who are properly briefed and given the right equipment; consequently, they are more likely to achieve their objective by following the agreed strategy and choice of tactics. In a negotiation choosing the right people with the right skills is part of the leader's responsibility. Choosing the team will therefore be a major consideration in the overall negotiation process.

TEAM

The team at minimum should consist of at least two people who are present on every occasion when there is an interaction between the parties. While there is no absolute maximum, more than five people in a negotiating team can prove difficult to manage as the company's position must remain consistent and should only be communicated with one voice. This is harder with so many people. In other words no matter what is discussed during a negotiation one person only should be authorized to make a definite statement to the counterparty which will become the statement from the company. This reinforces the need for the team to have a leader and only one leader.

The leader must have the authority of the CEO and/or the board to speak on behalf of the company and must manage the team and the negotiation on their behalf. For the smaller company this person may indeed be the CEO who has that authority. In a larger organization the negotiation ought to be led by a figure senior enough to carry that delegated authority. There are two main reasons for this, the first clearly being the need for experienced management of the process and the second is to avoid having to seek approval for every small step or change in direction that may occur during the negotiation process.

The remit given to the negotiating team must have clear objectives but sufficient latitude to be flexible in achieving the overall goal. This reminds me of an incident when we were pressed for better settlement terms on the eve of a major transaction by a third-party licensee from whom we required an assignment of rights to proceed with the larger transaction. I had been given the authority to negotiate terms up to a fixed ceiling of $7 million; the alternative, as the CEO starkly put it, being: 'Otherwise we'll sue them into the Dark Ages!' Although the negotiation took some time we got the assignment by offering a variety of payments and compensation options which avoided litigation and stayed in budget without further recourse to the CEO and his legal team.

Depending on the deal therefore there may be a need for a technical expert, a medical expert, legal representation but always, whenever negotiating, one person should be inactive in the discussion and have the role of recorder sometimes referred to as the 'scribe'. I was lucky enough to have a team member while at Roche who was qualified as an ethnologist (ethnology is a field closely associated with anthropology) and her abilities to study and record the interactions between people in a negotiation gave us a huge insight into not only what was being said but the importance that was assigned to it – on both sides of the table. So often she would point out in the debriefing after a negotiation session to one person or another that 'When you said "that" to the CEO on the other team he didn't react well to it, and he will reject that point later,' and sure enough despite having had agreement in the session we'd find that the issue she'd identified had indeed be rejected or modified in their response. Communication is much more complex than the mere verbal exchanges of a negotiation and since those days I have paid close attention to the reactions of other parties in a negotiation and to controlling the messages I send out both verbally and visually to good effect.

Documentation of the discussion in a negotiation ideally should not be restricted to the points which were agreed but should also track the decision process including the misunderstandings and corrections that led up to the agreement. The value of the scribe becomes even more apparent, in that, without a speaking part in the session, the scribe can concentrate on both the content of the discussion and how the discussion has developed. This almost always gives a different perspective to the recollection of the debate on one or other issue. There is an adage, 'when your mouth is open, your ears are closed,' which acknowledges that if you are talking, it is very difficult to listen to another person especially in a negotiation. Because a negotiation is not a conversation, every word counts. It is an exchange of statements where each party is trying to establish their point of view independently of the other. Each will therefore be looking for every chance to restate or re-affirm their point which detracts from their ability to hear the other perspective clearly.

OTHER ASPECTS OF PREPARATION

Preparation is therefore essential when approaching a negotiation, yet quite often some aspects are overlooked in the build-up and many of these factors are 'soft' in nature such as the location of the discussions. Frequently negotiations are held at the headquarters of one group or the other and from a logistics point of view this may seem sensible, yet it opens the door to a number of undesirable events. Many negotiations I have attended at small companies were plagued by interruptions as throughout the day the CEO or another person from the company had to break off discussions to deal with some business issue or another with the result that following the break a recap of the issues was required to return to the point at issue with a loss of continuity. Similarly the small company visiting the large partner may be the subject of interruptions giving the impression that they are not the focus of real attention and affect their motivation. Where it is possible the use of a neutral venue can avoid these problems and provide an environment where neither side is inconvenienced or advantaged by the other.

Another simple point is that presentations should be made and given that are adapted to the audience rather than being a standard 'pitch'. Too often the complaint is heard from one side or the other that they sat through a 30- or 40-minute dissertation of irrelevant material, or worse, hopped from one presentation to another because the information relevant to that meeting had not been collated into a coherent presentation. A practical advantage is provision of hard copies of the material as well as in electronic format – on the day – on CD, memory stick or similar device. This has increasingly become the standard of professional courtesy and if information is not provided this way it is seen as a negative point.

Yet with mention of the provision of materials we should revisit the issue of confidential disclosure agreements (CDAs) discussed in Chapter 5. Here when, at last, truly substantial issues are to be discussed, confidentiality must be assured and suitable undertakings should be exchanged if this has not already been completed. The proposal of terms and conditions for a commercial agreement are not trivial hence it is necessary here to step through the normal requirements of the term sheet and identify when and how these should be presented and discussed.

The purpose of a term sheet is to capture the essence of the proposed transaction in writing and to form the framework of the negotiation. The terms are stated in contract law and terms are those statements which are guaranteed to be true in the document. A condition is a specific form of term where the condition (such as a patent being issued) must be satisfied before the term becomes binding. Other conditions, such as a representation, may be stated by one of the parties but is not or cannot be guaranteed. There are also statements known as 'puffs' in contract law which are recognized as sales talk and are not regarded as being trustworthy, nor would the person uttering a puff be held to deliver on its promise in the way that an agreed term would be by a court of law. Hence in an offer of contract there may be puffs and

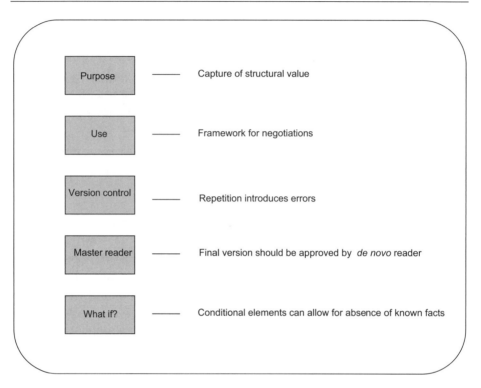

Figure 7.2   Term sheet issues

representations but it would not usually be possible to use these as grounds
for suing for breach of the contract if they were unfulfilled as they would not
be recognized as terms in the contract. So in creating a term sheet, statements
of those types are avoided and accurate descriptions and definitions used
instead. In effect the term sheet lays out the elements of a transaction in a
logical sequence and in a way that the parties can understand and agree on.
In the context of a pharmaceutical product licence the term sheet will fulfil at
least the following tasks:

- identify the contracting parties

- state the purpose of the contract

- identify the assets

- state the price to be paid and how

- state the duration of the contract

- state any contingencies or constraints.

The first term sheet is typically proposed by one of the parties as their preferred outcome to which the other side responds by either accepting or rejecting the proposal in whole or in part. So Company A might request of Company B:

> *'An exclusive, worldwide licence to Product X in perpetuity with the right to manufacture and develop the product further for a payment of $10 million and a following royalty of 5 per cent of net sales for 10 years.'*

This could lead Company B to respond that they would agree to an exclusive world licence to Product X but would retain manufacturing and development rights and want a payment of $25 million and a 15 per cent royalty for 20 years on gross sales.

These two positions are obviously far apart but has established that under acceptable conditions Company B is willing to license Product X to Company A on an exclusive worldwide basis if these can be negotiated. The process which follows may be rapid or can be long drawn out; counter-proposals may be exchanged frequently in an attempt to close the deal quickly or at long intervals as the internal valuations of the product's worth and the perception of the offer value fluctuate, or until other pressures alter the motivation of one or other of the companies.

During this process it is absolutely vital that there is a strong control of the printed versions of the term sheet which is being circulated and negotiated. It is time consuming, annoying and may even be the cause of failure in the negotiation if the negotiators and their colleagues are not all using the same version of the term sheet when considering and evaluating the terms. On each page of every iteration of the term sheet the date and serial number (such as V.1, 22 May 2008 and then V.2, 30 June 2008) should be in the header or footer of the document. At each negotiating session all the negotiators can then check that they are using the latest version for the next round. It is also useful to have the previous versions available for reference during these sessions as sometimes going back to a previous wording can recover a stalemate in the discussions and allow the deal to progress.

To ensure that each new version captures the points which have been agreed in the last negotiation session all participants should receive a marked-up copy of the last term sheet showing the changes that have been made and a draft of the fully revised version. These are frequently referred to as the 'black-line' and 'clean' copies respectively. Feedback on the clean copy from anyone requiring a change or inclusion of a missed point can then be incorporated for a final new version. Most word processing packages have a black line change-tracking facility which can produce these two versions easily. When using these packages, however, it is even more important to ensure that each changed document is saved with a new and distinctive file name for example, Productxdeal250707 V.2 including the deal name, version number and date. If more than one is produced in a day a suffix can be appended such as V2.3 which keeps a full record of the change history should things become confused.

Some of the terms in a term sheet may not, however, actually be known at the time the document is drawn up, particularly with compounds in development which in time might even be found not to work. These terms may therefore be conditional and describe the consequences for the contract for each of the cases envisioned as the possible outcomes. So although the terms of the contract will be binding, they do not have to be factually complete at the signing of the contract.

HOW TO SET ABOUT THE NEGOTIATION

Being unprepared is the worst thing to be in a negotiation. If you do not know what you want you cannot get it and will end up with what you get. If the other side has an objective and a plan you will end up in their back pocket. So, here are some practices that can help to set the scene for a negotiation.

The first is a technique known as 'anchoring'. This has been deeply studied by Daniel Kahneman, Nobel prizewinner for economics in 2002 and his work is far more extensive than what is discussed here. He presents an example of anchoring by asking an (US) audience to think of the last four digits of their social security number, and then to estimate the number of physicians in New York. The correlation between the magnitude of the social security number and the size of their estimate is around 40 per cent, a long way beyond a chance result. Simply thinking of the first number, large or small, biases the estimate of the second, even though there is no connection between them. In the same way it is possible for one negotiating team to influence the other by continually referring to another unrelated number, either higher or lower depending on the objectives. As this works in both directions you are able to set the tone of a negotiation merely by directing the 'ambient' frame of reference when you come to the negotiation of value, which you may wish to be high. Alternatively if you are setting the purchase price of supplies you are buying, a previous discussion of items in small numbers will be more appropriate. Subtle factors such as this have a great influence on the interaction between negotiators and so there is a need for constant vigilance to ensure that the signals you put out are under your control and that the ones you receive are recognized and allowed for in your interpretation. Here again the value of the scribe is evident: while as the negotiator you will be trying to remain detached from the emotional side of the interaction with your counterpart, it is rarely possible to remain quite so aloof, we are all human after all. Yet if through vigilance and subsequent analysis you can recognize the techniques being applied you can intellectually take them into account before making responses.

Erving Goffman, in his book *The Presentation of Self in Everyday Life*, has a lot to say about the control of responses individually and in teams. He uses the term 'performance team' to describe how groups of people establish roles in order to present a desired image or impression on others either individuals or teams. He gives the example of a medical team doing a ward round where the junior is required to read out the notes to the rest of the team in front of the patient, which demonstrates through his relative ignorance the learning of the professor and impresses the patient. In the same way the negotiating team needs to understand explicitly their individual roles in the negotiation team and present the correct image to elicit the right responses.

Once more the construction of the team is of great significance in this regard. The role of the scribe who stays quiet and takes no part in the active discussion, and the role of the leader who speaks with the authority of the company, have already been identified as major contributors to success. The team performance can be enhanced though by other members deliberately adopting roles which assist in this task. The occasion I mentioned earlier in this chapter, when I was invited to join a negotiation to perform one task which was to agree with the general manager, demonstrates this. So it is that in a series of negotiations it can be very useful to have one member who is continually asking ingénue questions, as if they don't understand, to force the other team into revisiting some point which does not suit your side and which you wish to pursue while the other team is trying to move on and avoid further discussion. In asking for a repetition quite often a different form of words may be used and this opens up the possibility of reinterpreting the point to your own advantage.

Having someone else to play this role therefore permits the leader to sit back and make the decision about when to say yes or no to a point, without having to demean his role by asking the naïve questions. Others may, intrinsically or by design, take up a challenging or belligerent attitude to disrupt the performance of the other team. Whichever way the performance is orchestrated and the roles apportioned, until the team has had a good deal of experience working together there will be a need to rehearse the negotiation performance just as a theatre group would rehearse before performing a play. Large companies have the advantage of staff dedicated to the task of negotiation and so these teams often build up good internal working relationships and a repertoire of roles to assist them in their performances. The professionalism which they can bring to a negotiation can be daunting for a smaller company. As a result, nowadays I am often called in to advise smaller companies on how to deal with a larger company team and assist their preparations and rehearsals, as their own limited resources must often be called in from their own specialists at short notice to avoid halting day-to-day business for the needs of the negotiation. The smaller company is usually at a huge disadvantage without this kind of preparation: they will only enter a negotiation once in a while but the large company team will be following a regular pattern. If the small company is poorly prepared they will have to deal with issues as they come up and improvise a response. Improvisation has a place, but is a higher-risk strategy than having a pre-planned objective. It is much easier to be deflected if you are not working to a plan with individual stepping stones toward your goal.

Building the team, briefing the team, assigning roles and rehearsing will make the negotiation in prospect more accessible, but as we are all aware the real world is less friendly than a rehearsal suite. Even if the whole performance of your team is a scripted game plan, it will be in danger if there are issues which have not been considered in putting the plan together. Having someone external to the project or the company offer a critique is a very useful discipline before commencing live negotiations. In cases where there is a great deal at stake companies can even engage in what are called 'war room simulations', a description drawn from the Cold War years in the United States when the nuclear response deterrent was frequently rehearsed in 'dry run' scenarios to practise responses to different attack scenarios. In a similar vein large companies, especially when considering major acquisitions, are known to construct two or more negotiation teams internally and have them perform mock negotiations from assumed starting points to see if there are flaws in their plans or where their tactics could lead them astray.

Not all negotiations are critical to the future of a company, yet negotiating skills are at the heart of every success and either a tough hard-nosed approach or a kid-glove seduction can achieve the business objective if they are deployed with premeditation and conviction.

What happens though if your negotiating stance is unattractive or ineffective? Or if you are placed in a competitive bidding situation? How do you regain traction on a deal which is getting away from you? How do you maintain momentum when the counterparty will not engage in a timely fashion? How do you negotiate from a position of weakness? All these questions are a matter of regular review throughout the negotiation process (see Figures 7.3 and 7.4).

In the negotiating room when things are not going to plan or initial expectation, one of the best responses is the 'time-out' or caucus. This gives the team a chance to get away from the table and compare notes. There is a risk in doing this that if things are going your way you will lose momentum, but if they are not it can be your chance to call a temporary halt and regroup. When the session recommences a quick recapitulation of the points leading up to the break and restating your case can give a negotiation a new start without loss of control. To facilitate this issue a secure and separate location should be provided for both of the teams as a part of the choice of venue, with Internet, fax and telephone communications facilities, as well as printers if possible for on-the-spot modifications, additions or changes of plan.

Do

- Anchor
- Meet in neutral areas
- Construct your team from the best
  (not those available or 'tourists')
- Run the show, be the boss
  (not a chairman)
- Document everything
- Communicate, 360 degrees

Figure 7.3   Do's in negotiations

Don't

- Allow side conversations, verbal or email
- Be inflexible, just stubborn
- Get dragged into side-issues
  - Stay focused on your plan
- Forget to listen
  - Repeat what they say

Figure 7.4   Don'ts in negotiations

Running a negotiation requires continual vigilance not just on the detail but on the wider scene. Good negotiators are usually those who keep an eye out for the unusual and are prepared to test the counterparty for not only weaknesses but for further opportunities. One of my favourite questions learned from my boss while in investing is 'What else?' At the end of most calls or meetings he would throw out this non-specific yet challenging question just to see if it produced a response. To him every conversation is like a negotiation and, until the answer to 'What else?' is 'Nothing', the deal isn't done.

Sealing the Deal: The Contract

Following the selection of a product and the proposals made to the owning company and having negotiated the terms to achieve a satisfactory deal for the components, these must now be captured in a contract which will allow the parties to achieve their objectives. In order to achieve this a document must be drawn up which is comprehensive and comprehensible to both parties. This is not easily achieved and so requires a great deal of skill. This is quite properly the province of a corporate contract lawyer; however, business development practitioners need to have sufficient awareness of the issues involved in contract law to be able to manage their negotiations to a point where the agreements they have made can be drafted accurately and then can be enacted in law. It is worth adding a disclaimer at this point that as a non-lawyer my views are open to wide interpretation; however, the following will I hope act as a loose guide for those of us who have not studied law formally.

Before plunging into the details of a contract it is worth understanding what the contract is and the following definition states the active principles in suitable legal language:

> *An agreement free from vitiating factors such as mistake or misrepresentation and constituted by the unconditional acceptance of an outstanding offer involving a reasonably precise set of terms between two or more contractually competent parties who intend to create mutual and reciprocal rights and duties that may be the subject of judicial sanction if they are expressed in any required form, are free from the taint of illegality or immorality and are not subsequently discharged by law, by agreement, by breach or by sufficient supervening circumstances.*

(The Canadian Encyclopedic Digest, 3rd edition)

Which I interpret as 'two parties agree to something reasonable which does not adversely affect other people'.

Contract structure

When an agreement is negotiated the terms and conditions may be complex and as a result sometimes even become inadvertently unenforceable or actually illegal. Adjustments to the agreements made in negotiation in normal English must therefore be made to permit a contract to be written. The method for achieving this as noted before requires a highly formalized structure. The analogy of a computer program can help to illustrate this point. A program written in a computer language such as Basic commences with a name for the program or routine and a description of its purpose. Following this are a series of declarations which identify the elements within the program, describing their name and type. These declared elements may then be included in programmatic statements contained in what is known as a subroutine using operators like +, -, *, /, and, or; each of which follow a structured grammatical language to provide a clear relationship between the elements which when computed produce a result. So it might run along the lines of what is presented in Figure 8.1.

There is a fixed relationship between these declared elements that is allowed to vary within certain defined parameters and can be used for reference to

```
Name 'Contract Program'
Rem  'Description: A series of statements to demonstrate the operation of a
contrast'
Rem 'Declarations'
Sales = Variable, Numeric
Term = Variable, Numeric
Payment = Constant, Numeric
Royalty = Variable, Numeric
Product = Constant, String
Licensor = Constant, String
Licensee = Constant, String

Sub
If
Licensee makes Payment to Licensor
for Product
then
if sales > 0
then
Royalty = 15%
end sub
end
```

Figure 8.1   A licensing 'program'

determine the result where ever required. Just as in a computer program where one subroutine can call another subroutine, the clauses within a contract which perform a task can call other clauses containing more terms into play. Indeed the analogy holds to the point where one contract can call on a different contract with its own special conditions to form an overall description of the operating relationship between two companies in for example a licence.

To get to this point the purpose of the contract (or contracts) must be declared. This will have been agreed in the term sheet discussions where the terms and conditions to be entered in the contract have been defined. This might be as simple as in this example reproduced in part here which is drawn from a real contract but modified to hide the actual companies and products.

LICENSE AGREEMENT

This LICENSE AGREEMENT ('Agreement'), effective as of May 17th, 1986, by and between SPROAT & COMPANY, an Arkansas corporation with its principal office located at Sproat Corporate Center, Rapid City, Arkansas 12345 ('Sproat'), and Origin8or, INC., a Delaware corporation with its principal offices located at 25 Ayrtech Court, Liberia, California 94123 and Origin8or's Affiliates (together 'Origin8or').

This tells us what the agreement is, who the parties are and, where they can be found as legal entities. We can then go on to look at the purpose, or as they're called in contract law, 'recitals', which is where the complexity of the contract starts in earnest. This is taken from the same contract:

RECITALS

1. WHEREAS, Sproat is engaged, among other things, in the business of discovering, developing, manufacturing and marketing pharmaceutical products for the treatment and prevention of infectious diseases;

2. WHEREAS, Sproat's research for antimicrobial agents has resulted in Sproat owning patents, patent applications and know-how relating to an mycocyllin B analog known as SP202255 (and analogs thereof);

3. WHEREAS, Sproat has been developing intravenous and oral formulations of SP202255 and generated regulatory filings, pre-clinical and clinical data and other information related to SP202255;

4. WHEREAS, Sproat is interested in exclusively licensing SP202255 to a pharmaceutical company capable and desirous of developing and commercializing both parenteral and oral pharmaceutical products of SP202255 (and/or analogs, salts or pro-drugs thereof);

---

5.   WHEREAS, Origin8or is a specialty pharmaceutical company which concentrates in the development and commercialization of compounds in the area of infectious diseases;

6.   WHEREAS, Origin8or has the capability and expertise to develop and commercialize both parenteral and oral pharmaceutical products;

7.   WHEREAS, Origin8or is interested in exclusively licensing rights to SP202255 from Sproat for the worldwide development and commercialization of both the parenteral and oral products of SP202255 (and/or analogs, salts or prodrugs thereof); and

8.   WHEREAS, subject to the terms and conditions set forth in this Agreement, Sproat is willing to exclusively license to Origin8or and Origin8or desires to exclusively license from Sproat rights related to SP202255 so that Origin8or may be enabled to proceed with the further development and commercialization of SP202255;

NOW, THEREFORE, the Parties hereto, intending to be legally bound, hereby agree as follows:

We cannot yet move onto the actual contract until the declarations or definitions have been made as they will be applied in the contract and this is achieved by clearly stating them, sometimes with negative examples to show what is NOT meant. These terms are set out in alphabetical order so that they can be referred back to by anyone reading the contract to ensure that the statement of terms is internally consistent.

The following definitions show several constructions demonstrating some of the difficulties encountered in defining an item accurately, completely and distinctly from other interpretations.

DEFINITIONS

1.1 DEFINITIONS. For purposes of this Agreement, the following terms shall have the meanings set forth below:

'AFFILIATES' shall mean, with respect to a Party to this Agreement, any Persons directly or indirectly controlling, controlled by, or under common control with, such other Person. For purposes hereof, the term 'controlled' (including the terms 'controlled by' and 'under common control with'), as used with respect to any Person, shall mean the direct or indirect ability or power to direct or cause the direction of management policies of such Person or otherwise direct the affairs of such Person, whether through ownership of equity participation, voting securities, beneficial interest, by contract or otherwise. Affiliate shall specifically exclude third parties to which Origin8or has granted a sublicense pursuant to authority granted by this Agreement where Origin8or has no relationship to the sublicensee other than a licensor–licensee relationship.

'APPLICATION FOR MARKETING AUTHORIZATION' shall mean (a) in the United States a new drug application filed with the FDA pursuant to 21 U.S.C. Section 357 and 21 C.F.R. Section 314 ('NDA') with respect to the Product and (b) in any country other than the United States, an equivalent application or set of applications for marketing approval comparable to an NDA necessary to make and sell Product commercially in such country.

'CO-PROMOTE' or 'CO-PROMOTION' shall mean an arrangement, in one or more jurisdictions where permitted, in which (i) there is a single registration holder for the Product; (ii) a single Party responsible for the manufacture of Product; (iii) a single Party establishing the price of Product; (iv) a single Party booking sales; (v) a single trademark being used in connection with the Product; (vi) both Parties promote and market sales of the Product in such jurisdiction(s); and (vii) either or both names or logos of the Parties appear on the Product.

'DAMAGES' shall mean any and all costs, losses, claims, liabilities, fines, penalties, damages and expenses, court costs, and reasonable fees and disbursements of counsel, consultants and expert witnesses incurred by a Party hereto (including any interest payments which may be imposed in connection therewith).

'DATA EXCLUSIVITY PERIOD' shall mean the period, if any, during which the FDA, or other equivalent regulatory agency in the case of countries other than the United States, prohibits reference, for purposes of seeking Regulatory Approval, to clinical and other data contained in the Regulatory Approval package of Origin8or or its sublicensee which is not published or publicly available outside of the Regulatory Approval package and relates to the Product, without the consent of the Party holding the NDA or equivalent Regulatory Approval.

'EFFECTIVE DATE' shall be the date set forth in the first paragraph of this Agreement.

'EUROPE' shall mean the European Union, including the following countries: Austria, Belgium, Denmark, Finland, France, Germany, Greece, Ireland, Italy, Luxembourg, Netherlands, Portugal, Spain, Sweden, United Kingdom and any other European Union countries at the time of the Effective Date.

'FDA' shall mean the United States Food and Drug Administration, or any successor thereto.

'FTE' shall mean the equivalent of the scientific work on or directly related to the Product of one scientific person full time for one year (consisting of a total of forty-seven (47) weeks or one thousand eight hundred eighty (1,880) hours per year) (excluding vacations and holidays).

'GAAP' shall mean generally accepted accounting principles in the United States, consistently applied.

These definitions in the example continue though the list of terms required to capture all the elements that will be needed to describe the contract.

'REIMBURSABLE DEVELOPMENT EXPENSES' shall mean all internal and external direct, actual and documented costs incurred by Origin8or after the Effective Date to develop the Oral Formulation of the Product, including, without limitation, pre-clinical and clinical trial expenses (including, without limitation, the direct cost of clinical trial materials), reasonable Third Party costs, Regulatory Approval expenses and fees, and costs associated with scientific personnel dedicated to development of the Oral Formulation of the Product, where scientific personnel costs shall be calculated at a rate of Two Hundred Thousand Dollars ($200,000) per FTE. The purchase of raw materials or supplies or external Third Party services shall be calculated using actual direct costs incurred by the Parties for such Third Party goods or services.

'RESERVE INVENTORY' shall mean Product Inventory which is not being purchased by Origin8or as of the Effective Date and which is specifically identified as Reserve Inventory in EXHIBIT D attached hereto.

'ROW' shall mean all the countries and territories of the world, except those in North America and Europe.

'ROYALTY TERM' shall mean, with respect to each country in which Product is sold the period of time equal to the longer of (i) ten (10) years from the date of first sale of the Product in such country, (ii) the expiration of the last-to-expire Licensed Patent listed in EXHIBIT A in such country that claims such Product, or (iii) the period of time equal to the Data Exclusivity Period in such country.

'START-UP INVENTORY' shall mean Product Inventory which is being purchased by Origin8or as of the Effective Date of this Agreement and which is specifically identified as Start-Up Inventory in EXHIBIT D attached hereto.

'TERRITORY' shall mean all the countries and territories of the world.

'TRANSFERRED ASSETS' shall mean the Start-Up Inventory and the Product Data Package.

'ORIGIN8OR CO-PROMOTION RIGHT' shall have the meaning set forth in Section 3.4(f).

'ORIGIN8OR IMPROVEMENTS' shall mean any inventions, patentable or not, information and/or data that are generated, identified and/or discovered by Origin8or during the term of the Agreement, based on use or practice of the Licensed Patents or Licensed Technology, and are related to the Product, including, without limitation, pre-clinical studies and clinical trial information, manufacturing processes, formulations, modes of delivery and/or data necessary for the manufacture, use or sale of the Product, or peripheral and/or SAR compounds, pharmaceutical compositions, manufacturing processes, product configurations and methods of use related to the Licensed Patents.

'ORIGIN8OR RESPONSIBILITIES' shall have the meaning set forth in Section 3.1 hereof.

The material given in example has had its details changed to protect anonymity but has been taken from a real contract. The definitions used and their structure are entirely typical of licence contracts enacted in the United States and in most jurisdictions where common laws and contract laws are based on English Law. The degree of detail permits almost no misinterpretation, so when these definitions are used in the context of the contract their meaning can be referred to at any time by looking at the definitions section the contract. Contracts drawn up under other European country laws by contrast have historically often not been so detailed. This had led to wider interpretations when disputes occur, especially where the parties to the contract are from different countries and legal jurisdictions and may not have understood the implications of the agreement they have made. The trend now is to follow a more Americanized model and often to draft contracts in English even when they are enacted between companies neither of whom have English as their mother tongue. Litigation, or the threat if it, in the pharmaceutical industry sadly is increasingly being used as a negotiation ploy rather than a last resort and the protections that a solid and well-worded contract provides is the first line in establishing the rights and duties of the parties.

Other contract types such as clinical study agreements, distribution agreements and supply agreements each have their own standard forms.

The sample contract I have used to illustrate definitions continues for another 25 pages and includes sections titled as follows:

1. GRANT OF LICENSES, TRANSFER OF TRANSFERRED ASSETS AND ASSUMPTION OF LIABILITIES

2. PAYMENTS

3. TERM OF AGREEMENT

4. ADDITIONAL COVENANTS AND AGREEMENTS OF THE PARTIES

5. INTELLECTUAL PROPERTY MANAGEMENT

6. INDEMNIFICATION

7. TERMINATION

8. MISCELLANEOUS

Drafting the contract

It is not the aim of this chapter to explain in detail every part of a contract but to describe the structure of the document in sufficient depth to indicate its use in the general run of business. What this example does illustrate very clearly is the absolute reliance of the business development function and the company as a whole on well-qualified and experienced legal advice. In contract law the meaning of each word or phrase has a particular and specific significance and when dealing with international transactions every contract needs to be checked for its validity and enforceability in each individual jurisdiction where the companies will be relying on it to protect their businesses. While this process should not be undertaken by non-professionals, as the probability of making costly mistakes is extremely high, the governance of the process needs to be managed by the business development function whether they are legally qualified or not.

During the drafting of such a contract there needs to be very close collaboration between the legal department and the business development group with close management of the inputs of each individual specialist into the components of the contract. Ensuring that the overall scope of the contract captures the negotiated points, however, must remain the responsibility of the business development department. Unless the contract reflects the agreements made and continues to do this through successive drafts, the spirit of the agreement will be lost. Unfortunately, some legal departments have been known to try and seek to improve the conditions of a contract by careful use of drafting language. It may even be that substantial changes are made by an overzealous legal department in an effort to please management. In fact recently one of my own advisory contracts was returned by a legal department after I had agreed terms with the CEO in which the redraft of my proposed contract doubled the period of my engagement, halved the fee and introduced a performance component of no relevance to the task all with no reference to either myself or the CEO! While this example was blatant on numerous occasions legal redrafting of a more subtle nature either in the definitions or deep in the clause structure has deliberately been used to distort the agreed business terms beyond recognition. Oversight is required to preserve and maintain not only the facts but the truth of the negotiation.

Prior to the drafting of such a contract the parties will have agreed the substance of the term sheet and may choose to execute a letter of intent which will bind the parties to the execution of a contract during the period while the contract is being drafted. As may be seen from the complexity of the example shown in this chapter, this process can take many weeks if not months to complete. In the interim the Letter of Intent (LOI) can secure the interests of both parties and permit the transaction to be brought to an orderly close without undue haste. However, there are occasions when there is a need to close a deal more rapidly. For instance this might be to meet the end of a financial year, or to beat out a competitor, or to benefit from taxation regulations. In these cases there are several things which deserve particular attention in order not to be overlooked. The most critical of these is to ensure that a schedule of required documentation is laid out before the closing approaches and that therefore all contracts, subsidiary agreements, permissions, liens, assignments and waivers are executed. This needs to be recorded by the legal department and the completed schedule overseen by business development to ensure that all rights and titles are transferred on or by the closing date.

Of particular importance in perfecting a product licensing deal are the re-registrations of marketing authorizations, clinical trial certificates and the like. Moreover, the wave of regulatory fallout from a transaction needs to be pursued across the globe to ensure there is no possibility of a territory being left out and generic competition being commenced through an oversight. This kind of problem was highlighted for some companies after Malta acceded to the European Union: they had not considered the possibility 20 years before that such a small state would become an independent member of the EU and had therefore had not registered their products there. This has permitted a burgeoning generic industry to spring up with the right to distribute its products throughout the EU. The number of states in the EU was 27 in 2007 and is likely to continue to increase as accession states qualify for membership. It is to be hoped that legal departments will also have taken note of the recent independence of Montenegro and of other small Balkan states and will not have made a similar error regarding product and patent registrations.

Closing can be impeded unless attention to detail is paid to issues such as inventory management, noted before; whether the inventory is cGMP (clinical Good Manufacturing Practice) materials for clinical trials, batches of finally manufactured product, components or packaging materials. All inventory covered by an agreement should be accounted for by physical checking not just a paper check. Any of these items can become 'lost' temporarily or permanently during a change of ownership unless the receiving party is completely vigilant in ensuring that the transfer is effected and this will require warehouse visits to verify the existence of the physical stock, the amount, that the materials are in date and not subject to spoilage.

If there are outstanding issues post-closing and an escrow account has been set up to remedy discrepancies or defaults, the contract or subcontract needs to be utterly explicit in its interpretation of when, what and how a default, a breach, or transgression is constituted, and how the trigger will be signalled to the counterparty and the remedy will be applied. Naturally this implies that as the transaction progresses the business development group will take an active part in ensuring that both parties comply with the terms of the contract. How long this should remain the responsibility of the business development department and when the project can be taken over by operational management will depend very much on the complexity of the transaction and the tenor of the closing. If all is settled on congenial terms there should be fewer concerns to be monitored. A toughly negotiated transaction with contentious issues or disaffected personnel on either side will require periodic or more frequent scrutiny.

Making the Transaction Work

CHAPTER

9

The nature of the alliance

The structure of an alliance results in large part from the differences or similarities of the partners in size, financial capacity and strength of portfolio. This leads to relationships which are either dominant/subordinate or peer to peer in nature. The symmetry of the partnership at the highest level will have a strong influence on how the alliance needs to be managed at a personal level. As has been noted elsewhere the culture of bigger companies tends to induce some managers to role play the self-important bully when dealing with their partners merely because of the size of the company they work for and this can have very negative effects on the outcome of the alliance if it is allowed to disturb its work. Strong leadership in an alliance needs to be tempered by a sense of duty to a smaller or less experienced partner to obtain the best results. Observing the interactions between the managers is a good way of diagnosing whether an alliance is working well or not. An alliance which is suffering tensions between the respective managers is unlikely to be as productive as one where good leadership skills are being practised.

Motivations for forming an alliance are expressions of the strategy adopted by both companies. For an alliance to succeed the combination of the strategic intents of the partners has to make sense. These typically fall into one of three categories: defensive, offensive or discovery.

A large company may need to shore up its development pipeline or reinforce its sales abilities in a specific territory. In these situations being able to avoid having to take the time required to recruit and train staff or to bring a product from research into the clinic has major attractions. Forming an alliance with a partner that has the needed resources is a defensive move which makes a great deal of sense. This may be true of the partner as well where a pooling of resources gives protection from competition or erosion of the number of patented products in the portfolio. Alternatively the partners may have an offensive or more aggressive ambition in mind having seen a market opportunity which together they can attack although alone neither would be likely to succeed. Whatever the motivation, such an alliance has to bring benefits to both partners to make commercial sense. A company motivated by discovery, however, will expand its existing capabilities and venture into new areas. Smaller and earlier-stage companies have fewer constraints with regard to experimentation in novel therapies as their focus is to innovate, larger companies although they have less financial constraint need to produce a reliable source of income. So it is no surprise to see large companies taking advantage of their strength and partnering with successful pioneers in Biotech.

Alliances are often aimed at the three key areas of the business; research, development and commercial (see Figure 9.1).

It is in these areas that the core competencies of an individual company can be augmented most easily and have a major impact on the success of a project or the company as a whole. A company would not typically enter an alliance to improve its administration functions. Under these three broad headings subsets of activity can be the focus of an alliance and these may be further allied in a network of partnerships all aimed at achieving one objective. This network may be organized as a consortium of companies with multilateral relationships each to the other or may be linked through one company in a 'hub and spoke' arrangement where the overall project is coordinated by one, usually the largest, company (see Figure 9.2).

In sales for instance several distributors may be appointed for different countries and centrally supplied with products. In development, companies may band together to share the tasks of process development, formulation and clinical research. Discovery research is clearly an area where cooperation and

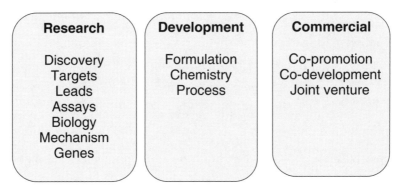

Figure 9.1   Alliance types

Alliances

- Bi-lateral

- Multi-lateral

- 'Hub and spoke'

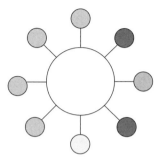

Figure 9.2   Alliance structures

collaboration with partners is a benefit, not just because of the savings in costs of time and money but for the combination of ideas from different sources to address a research target. Bilateral alliances also offer companies the chance to access key technologies which they do not or cannot own.

Making the alliance work

The conclusion of the contract was at one time the signal for business development to step out of the transaction and return to the market for more deals. This is no longer the case. The imperative now is to provide a partnering environment where small and large companies can benefit from the transaction and complete the development of the drug, or integrate the acquisition. Following the acquisition of Boehringer Mannheim by Roche in 1997 I was involved in the considerable programme of integration which followed the closing of the transaction. A year later the press was commenting on how smooth this had been by comparison with other large M&A deals at the time. What we had learned from that period was that planning is of the most importance in such an undertaking and this large part came from the, at that time, still recent corporate memory of the takeover of Syntex.

Only a few companies have the benefit of frequent experience in M&A, which permits the creation of a set of guiding principles learned from each integration of a company and can be implemented from one transaction to the next. The consequence of this is that the executives undertaking the transaction are put in the position of being 'first-timers' and so lack the reflexes to make quick but correct decisions. Business development typically has to deal with new, or at least unfamiliar, situations every day in evaluating novel opportunities. How then to translate the experience of one situation to another and maintain a consistent approach?

New situations require a structured approach and useful parallels to an unstable business environment are provided by the problems encountered in flying a light aeroplane and in scuba-diving where unfamiliar events often occur and require a trained, structured approach to handle them and sometimes survive them. Pilots and divers are trained to follow simple but effective guidelines which lead to courses of action which have been worked out by trial and error over years of handling problems to give the best result in an emergency. One of the most notable of these is a very useful acronym used to assist in a crisis: PAPA – or Pause, Assess, Plan, Act. The deliberate act of acquiring a company may not sound like a crisis but for two large organizations to be brought together without 'crashing' their cultures or operational effectiveness takes on the same kind of urgency. As in the air or under the sea, problems will crop up for the first time in the experience for the manager once a takeover has occurred. The problems may be in manufacturing standards, clinical data records, accounting procedures, some ongoing litigation or other special situations where the normal practices in the acquired company are alien to the new owner, who will need to rapidly assimilate, understand and decide on a course of action and literally 'take over the reins' of the new company and try not to fall off the horse. PAPA is an excellent aid to good planning in situations such as M&A and alliance creation and management where, despite good planning, the unexpected is almost sure to happen.

PAUSE

Unless there is some immediate crisis requiring an instant decision there is almost no excuse for jumping into action before it is needed. Many of the leaders I have worked with had the characteristic of not being easily rushed into a decision. Early in my career at G.D. Searle UK, the marketing manager Brian Moyse would often demonstrate *sang froid* in the face of a crisis and usually the problem would resolve itself before any action was needed. This was an excellent lesson for a young manager in the art of pausing.

ASSESS

Gathering the facts is of paramount importance before any action. There are many proverbs and sayings – look before you leap, a stitch in time, and so on which have made this point. What looks like a problem may not be that at all when viewed coolly and with all the facts at hand. Often an impending worry looks worse than it is in reality and may be a caused by a 'mirage' of misunderstanding, which reinforces the need for the pause and a clear determination of the facts.

If there is a problem, finding out how it came about and how it may be resolved can only be determined from assessing the facts. So the crucial skill in the assessment is asking questions and building up a mental picture of the issues. As discussed before in the section on negotiation in Chapter 7, gathering information into a mind map can assist the process. It can also help to communicate the problem to others, especially those who would like to 'step-in' and take charge for their own reasons.

PLAN

Having taken the time to confirm a problem exists and having determined why and how it came about the opportunity exists to create a plan which will be appropriate, timely and thorough. The latter point is the most important as the thoroughness of the plan will mean the action taken will follow through to take care of side issues and so be more than a quick fix.

ACT

After the brief hiatus of the pause a proper review of the facts, and the creation of the plan to deal with the main issue and its side effects, it will be possible to take action which can be decisive, comprehensive and appropriate to the task.

The combination of this simple sequence can be a powerful ally during the cut and thrust of a transaction particularly after the execution of the contract when a series of events will rapidly unfold, a number of which will not have been foreseen prior to the closing. But it is at this point that the management of an alliance starts to take effect, and the essential feature of an alliance is that it is a dynamic relationship between two partners; it should not rely upon one party enforcing its rights under contract without the complicity and compliance of the other. In order to gain these the structure of the contract, while precise in its language, should not be so inflexible that it cannot accommodate to changes in circumstances. In order to achieve this, there must be a method of governance for the alliance with suitable representation from both sides.

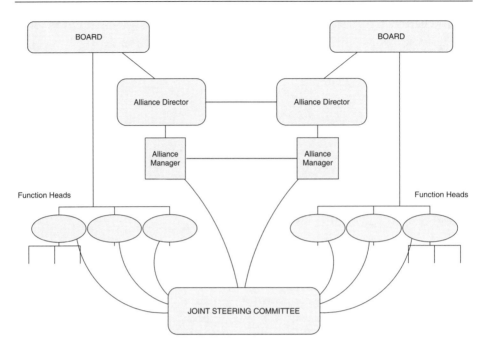

Figure 9.3   Joint steering committee

Alliance management

THE JOINT STEERING COMMITTEE

The most common structure in a licensing agreement to deal with matters of governance requiring decisions which involve both parties is a joint steering committee. The structure of such a committee and the voting rights will be stated in the contract and it is commonly the case that the senior partner will usually have a casting vote when the committee comes to a split decision. Most often the committee will be working towards a single purpose and disputes will not arise, however there can be occasions, particularly where details of a strategy have not been foreseen, when one partner needs to take the lead. Seniority in such cases is typically a function of the amount of finance provided to a transaction, but can sometimes be a retained right of the patent holder especially when other indications are to be developed for the molecule involved. The committee will meet regularly on a fixed schedule to review project progress and the achievement of results. Where the project involves a clinical development programme, the committee may also oversee the clinical development plan and individual clinical trial designs and their presentation to the regulatory authorities.

THE ALLIANCE MANAGER

The joint steering committee is not intended to manage the alliance on a day-to-day basis. That responsibility will lie with the project leader, or leaders, depending upon the scale of the relationship. Quite often larger companies will appoint an alliance manager to whom several project managers may report. The alliance manager's role will also be defined closely in the contract and in everyday business the alliance manager will have the delegated authority of the joint steering committee. Individual project managers in such functions as manufacturing, development, regulatory affairs, or medicinal chemistry will pursue their tasks in their own teams and follow the overall project plan under the guidance of the alliance manager.

The alliance manager role, however, extends beyond the maintenance of a project plan and reporting to the steering committee. They will typically also have an internal reporting line to management within their own company. The purpose of this reporting line is to ensure that the goals of the individual company are satisfied in the achievement of the project objectives and the maintenance of the relationship with the partner. The relationship needs to be sponsored at many different levels as will the peer-to-peer relationships between scientists and other functional staff. These will be complemented by financial relationships managed through the corporate finance function and management relationships beyond the joint steering committee which address the common objectives of the two companies as well as their individual agendas.

Successful alliance management is characterized by strong communication skills and links, frequent interaction and the building up of trust. Emphasis needs to be put on communication and documentation as these are crucial elements in successful alliance management. The need for coordination is uppermost in such complex relationships which may involve multi-site or multi-country interactions. Use of video conferencing and teleconferencing facilities, together with intranet or extranet connections, enhance the capabilities of alliance teams dramatically by providing the opportunity for personal interactions on a frequent basis without the need for constant travel. It is nevertheless the case that inter-site visits will continue to be a mainstay of alliance management. No matter how efficient electronic communications are, the need for individuals to meet, exchange ideas and become friends cannot be ignored. When two teams are expected to work together over many years, meeting in person is an important component of interpersonal relationships. As a result the social aspects of an alliance can become some of its greatest strengths.

Investment in alliances is one of the major success factors of modern pharmaceutical business, each of the larger companies can boast well over 50 continuing alliances at any one time; a major commitment of people and resources over and above the internal research and development obligations. This reflects the focus of an industry where innovation is the only justification for premium pricing and the pursuit of innovative medicines is the single most sustainable route to continuing profitability. Without the ability to establish and maintain effective alliances large-scale pharmaceutical endeavours would founder. Honing the skills required for managing alliances is therefore an integral part of business development in the twenty-first century.

Dealing with problems in alliances

Unfortunately not all alliances proceed according to plan; throughout the course of an alliance which could last 5 or 7 years personnel will change, objectives will alter and science will advance. Consequently there will be plenty of opportunities for changes of heart, changes of mind, misunderstandings and good old fashioned mistakes. Alongside possible strategic changes of direction at some point there are likely to be disagreements in interpretation of results and a consequent dispute about the appropriate next steps and which direction to take. The joint steering committee has the task of arbitrating issues that cannot be resolved at team level. As noted above the committee will normally have the right to decide issues by vote and in the case of a tie the casting vote will go to the senior partner. However, it may be that the joint steering committee itself adopts a position which the management one of the partners finds unacceptable and therefore puts it in conflict with its partner under the terms of the contract.

Although such conflict can arise from any one of a number of sources, conflicts can be resolved with little difficulty if a formula for bringing about a resolution has been put in place beforehand. Lack of such a mechanism can lead to a cascade of disharmony following a path which can end either in disengagement, renegotiation, arbitration, litigation or finally termination.

DISENGAGEMENT

Disengagement usually comes about as a result of issues which arise from external constraints and not through the fault of either of the parties. It might be that a competitor invalidates a patent involved in the project, or perhaps produces a superior product which removes the potential value of the asset.

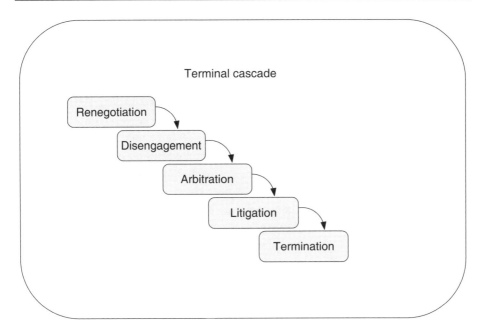

Terminal cascade

Renegotiation

Disengagement

Arbitration

Litigation

Termination

Figure 9.4   The terminal cascade

In either of these cases pursuit of the development may become irrelevant to the business case of one or other partner. Alternatively the asset itself may not perform well in the clinic or may be found to have long-term toxicity problems. This last issue is the most common reason for disengagement of parties in an alliance and is usually dealt with by following the course set down in the contract for that eventuality.

There might be cases where force majeure prevents successful completion of an alliance. Examples of this are a natural disaster or the revolutionary change of government in a country. The decision to disengage and end the contract in cases of this kind would be taken independently by the managements of the companies and a proposal would be drawn up by one or other to abandon the agreement. If there were to be any persisting value to one of the partners in the IP or in any of the work conducted during the alliance then the proposal might include an offer for those rights. The essential aim in circumstances of this kind is that the situation is amicably resolved through discussion and a joint decision is made. Following a resolution of this kind where the outcome is suitable to both parties a joint press release is often made to note the passing of the alliance with guidance for the financial community.

RENEGOTIATION

Where there is some disagreement between the parties there may be a need to renegotiate the terms of the contract to reflect changes in circumstances, especially if there is a shift in the value of the opportunity in favour of one party over the other. This happened to me once when a chance finding came to light and altered the course of one of our alliances. Information which emerges from the market about a product may have major positive or negative implications, and I was standing with the head of research at a company get-together when one of the therapeutic area heads from research came over with a fax which had been received from an investigator in the US. The investigator had received sponsorship from our US affiliate to conduct a study using one of our products. The results of the study he had found so exciting that he had immediately sent a fax of the results graph to the head of the research group and sure enough we could all see that the product was highly effective in treating a serious disease and would have a major market potential. Yet there was no mention of this disease in the contract between ourselves and the patent holder. What was immediately required was a revision to the contract to capture this new opportunity.

Novel indications have quite often been discovered through experimental use of products by curious or inventive physicians and this can cause contractual difficulties for the partners engaged in marketing the product if it has been licensed in for one use alone. Alternatively a company's rights to a product can alter radically in the event that they are the subject of a takeover by agreement or as a result of a hostile bid. In the event that your alliance partner is acquired by a competitor, renegotiation of the contract may need to be urgently undertaken. Even if a change of control clause in the contract already assigns options to the parties in such an event, the actual circumstances may dictate a different course.

Another frequent cause of the need for a renegotiation is when delays to the regulatory submission, or regulatory approval for a product, remove the commercial incentive for continuing the alliance completely or requires additional funding for more clinical studies to support the submission, which may be a major disincentive to the partners. In either case the contract will need to be amended accordingly. Methods for achieving this include an addendum or codicil to the contract which can be used to take the special circumstance into account. On a more positive note, as in the event of a new indication, it may be that a side contract can deal with the new circumstances without there being any need to alter the original contract. However, if the changes required are of major extent or would so imbalance the original contract, a full renegotiation and redrafting of the original may be necessary.

ARBITRATION

Inevitably there will be some contractual situations where disputes arise due to some perceived or real default on the part of one of the parties. When there is no clear path to a resolution through negotiation because the disagreement is sufficiently intractable, one recourse is to arbitration. In most contracts the potential for such a deadlock is recognized by a clause which is inserted to specify both the authority which under whose jurisdiction the arbitration will be heard, the location of the hearings, in which language they will be heard and under the laws of which country.

These often tie in with the chosen authority but some exceptions are possible, and they can be highly significant as I encountered whilst advising a client recently.

A dispute had arisen with a larger company over the reporting of work completed under a research contract. As a result the larger company had refused to pay for work which had been undertaken because they had not been informed of progress according to the contract schedule, despite evidence that the work had been completed. In fact the dispute was motivated not by an operational problem but by the desire of the larger company to obtain control of the IP without paying for it. The contractual stratagem they were using to force the issue with my client was to withhold payment for the completed work, placing my client under severe financial pressure.

Things were not looking good until we examined the contract and found that when it had been written the arbitration clause had specified Copenhagen as the place, under Danish law. When my client realized this they were able to take a stand and refuse to be bullied by these 'strong-arm' tactics. They offered to defend their position by invoking the arbitration clause. Faced with this turn of events the aggressor company realizing that the case would have to be heard in Danish, had second thoughts. As they were a Delaware-based company the fact that they would have to physically be represented in Copenhagen and conduct the case in Danish immediately changed their attitude. Not long after this they made an approach through a third party to settle the dispute amicably. This was the path that was followed and the bills were settled just in time to save my client's business.

Companies seem quite often to agree to terms at the initiation of an alliance with little thought to the consequences of a real dispute occurring and an oversight of that kind can be the undoing of careful planning with serious consequences when it comes to a dispute. In this case it was perhaps also poetic justice that the larger company's use of the contract as a subterfuge was undermined by the fact that they had not bothered to read the contract to the end and suffered the consequences. Needless to say the atmosphere in this alliance moved from an open cooperative relationship to one of suspicion, distrust and protectionism which will inevitably lead to a dissolution of the alliance. Yet without the safety net of the arbitration things could have been worse.

When a case proceeds all the way to an arbitration it needs to be recognized that the arbitrator takes evidence in exactly the same way as any court would. Consequently the preparation of an arbitration needs as much care as any other civil suit. The grounds must be established, the evidence gathered, the documentation located and the witnesses selected. When it comes to the presentation of the case it is necessary to be willing to last the course and to pursue your interests to a final conclusion. It is also worth remembering that arbitrators are not just there to examine the contract and decide the case on points of law: they may be swayed by the credibility of witnesses and can find for one side or the other on more than legal grounds only, especially when it comes to the judgment and the awarding of compensation or damages, and to ruling on issues of ownership or fault. This can mean that at least one of the protagonists may be unhappy with the result of the arbitration and wish to appeal the decision. As long as is it has been provided for in the contract there will be a right of appeal should the arbitration be inequitable to one partner or the other. If the contract can require that the arbitrator's decision must be accepted as final, any decision to go to arbitration needs to be weighed very carefully and other negotiated options considered. A negotiated settlement is always preferable, and arbitration and litigation should be the last resorts of any dispute resolution process.

LITIGATION

In the final analysis, if one party believes it has been significantly disadvantaged by the other and has had damage caused to its business through major abuse of its IP or breaching of exclusive contractual rights, it may be that litigation is the only suitable course remaining. Needless to say litigation is not a trivial matter: the costs can be extremely high and the result of a defended case will always be in some level of doubt.

If there is no alternative to litigation certain issues need to be borne in mind. Firstly, who is the defendant and who the plaintiff? A significant burden of proof and what are called 'sufficient' grounds are required to instigate litigation. This is intended to prevent spurious or frivolous suits being brought about by companies jockeying for competitive advantage through the practice of launching a suit against another company. This has become seen much more often and this trend looks set to continue. The corollary of this trend is that all companies engaging in alliances need to be prepared, and to be prepared means rigorous attention to the creation, execution and operation of the alliance contracts.

In preparing a case there are great many issues to be decided much of which can only be evaluated on the advice of legal counsel. Depending on the legal advice about the grounds for the case, the defendant may be able to challenge the suit and force a change in jurisdiction or from one level of court to another, from district to state (or vice versa) or to the judge's chambers for summary judgement – any of which may improve their chances of prevailing. In the same way the legal advisors may be able to modify the choice of suit to be presented or defended by negotiation with opposing counsel or with the court to improve the chances of success.

Within the choice of suit as noted above is the choice of grounds for bringing the case. Some grounds may be stronger than others (meaning more likely to win the case) but the victory may provide less relief from the cause of the suit, such as a temporary injunction rather than a permanent one. The choice of grounds is therefore usually made on the basis of a higher likelihood of success rather than extracting the maximum punitive result. Another aspect of prime importance is the presentation of the case. The choice of witnesses can be highly significant; experts can assist if they are persuasive and well versed but can be a hindrance if they are poorly organized or uncertain in their presentation, particularly under cross-examination.

It is also worth bearing in mind that when engaged in litigation the legal team for the opposition has a right to information to present their case. This can mean that in accepting the defence of a case you concede the right for the plaintiff's lawyers to enter your offices and make copies of any information in your files even though you may consider this commercially sensitive, confidential or even private. In certain legal jurisdictions it is perfectly permissible to admit into evidence handwritten marginal notes made by attendees at meetings, whether on scratch pads or presentation notes. If these were to include personal observations regarding a member of the other party's delegation this may be offered as evidence of an antagonistic attitude. There have even been instances where extensive doodles on the meeting notes of one of the attendees have been presented as evidence that the meeting was not being taken seriously! This kind of evidence collection and utilization is a warning to us all to be extremely careful in our approach to business development negotiations. Unprofessional acts have a nasty habit of being exposed and being used in evidence.

As noted above, when a judgment is rendered it may satisfy one or other of the parties or indeed neither. Courts of justice will rule on points of law and on the judge's opinion. If the case brought before it is thought to be spurious, weak or malicious this may result in an unsatisfactory judgment or the case might be dismissed entirely, preventing further legal action. This is part of the risk in undertaking litigation as the protagonists will have involved a third party whose interests are not aligned with either of their own.

If allowed by the court an appeals procedure is often pursued and yet again there must be sufficient grounds for such an appeal. This whole process can swallow up time and expense to an enormous degree – even to the point where the litigation overshadows the business of the company. Some companies have become notorious in business development circles for their rapid and ready resort to law to solve their problems or disrupt the business of competitors. It would be nice to think that these practices will not proliferate further but in view of the litigious hostilities between research-based companies and generic manufacturers this is not possible. The battlefront is entrenched and the law is the primary means of attack and defence.

TERMINATION

When all else has failed the means to terminate an alliance, a licence or a contract should be provided for by a termination clause.

As observed before, a benign requirement for termination of a contract might be when the scientific evidence no longer supports the continued development of the product. Both parties will regretfully conclude that there is no future in the alliance and that the best course of action is to trigger the termination clause by mutual consent. Another significant cause of the terminations of alliances is a change of priorities in a big pharmaceutical company. This is frequently the result of a change in the perceived value of the product. If, for instance, the results of a Phase II study demonstrate that the product has some safety concerns which will limit the number of patients for whom it may be used, or if in a Phase III study the efficacy is found to be less than the target product profile (restricting the claims that could be made for the product, and so its likelihood of receiving reimbursement by health-care providers) then continued investment in the product will no longer makes sense. In such a case a unilateral termination of the contract may be initiated and the licensed rights returned to the originating company.

It is typical to find clauses in contracts between larger and smaller companies which provide a 'step-out' of the alliance contracts for the larger company with minimal obligations. These are usually a prerequisite in alliances where proof of concept is needed to proceed with the product development. The change of control provisions discussed earlier are also a form of step-out trigger and are a regular cause of alliance terminations. However it is also not unusual to find that this is expressed as an option to terminate rather than as an automatic event. The company can choose to exercise this right but is more likely to use the opportunity to seek to renegotiate its rights in an attempt to achieve better conditions or terms in the alliance agreement.

When considering termination certain pitfalls need to be avoided. These can include persisting rights to assets or non-terminating contractual obligations. Wherever possible the termination of a contract should be by agreement of both parties and whenever undertaken all documentation of the termination of the transaction should be archived. By archiving the data properly with full cross-referencing of documents later disputes or due diligence by potential acquirers can be facilitated and act as a protection against claw-backs to cover persistent obligations.

As this book goes to press the recent rulings by the US Supreme Court on the KSR vs Teleflex case has altered the landscape once more. This ruling changes the accepted definition of 'obviousness' in a patent claim. This will have a major impact pharmaceutical alliance management. The KSR vs Teleflex case has been magnified in its importance by another case in 2007, Medimmune vs Genentech, which establishes the right of a licensee to challenge the licence contract without the need for a breach of contract to have occurred. The combination of these two rulings will have far reaching effects and must be urgently addressed for both existing and new alliance contracts.

Glossary

A61K	patent application for medical, dental or toiletry purposes
ACE	acetyl cholinesterase
ADME	absorption distribution metabolism excretion
ADMET	absorption distribution metabolism excretion and toxicity
ANDA	abbreviated new drug application
API	active product ingredient
ASCO	American Society of Clinical Oncology
ASH	American Society of Hematology
Big pharma	larger pharmaceutical companies
BIO	Biotech Industry Organization
Biotech	biotechnology
Blockbuster	sales in excess of $1 billion per annum
CAT	Cambridge Antibody Sciences plc
CDA	confidential disclosure agreement
CEO	chief executive officer
CFO	chief financial officer
cGMP	clinical Good Manufacturing Practice
CMC	chemistry, manufacturing and controls
CoGs	cost of goods
COX2	clyclo-oxygenase 2 Inhibitors
DataMonitor	Datamonitor Europe plc
ECBD	European Course on Biobusiness Development
ECPM	European Center for Pharmaceutical Medicine
EFB	European Federation of Biotechnology
EMEA	European Agency for the Evaluation of Medicinal Products
EVCA	European Venture Capital Association

FDA	US Food and Drug Administration
FT	*Financial Times*
GATT	General Agreement on Trade and Tariffs
GERD	gastro esophageal reflux disease
GMP	good manufacturing practice
GPS	global positioning system
IMS	Intercontinental Medical Statistics Inc.
IPO	initial public offering
IPR	intellectual property rights
IT	information technology
LBO	leveraged buy-out
LES	Licensing Executives Society
LOI	letter of intent
M&A	mergers and acquisitions
MBO	management buy-out
MCA	Medicines Control Agency
MHRA	Medicine and Healthcare products Regulatory Authority
MS	multiple sclerosis
MTA	material transfer agreement
NDA	new drug application
NDA	non-disclosure agreement
NIH	US National Institutes of Health
NSAID	Non-steroidal anti-inflammatory drugs
OTC	over the counter non-prescription medicines
PAPA	pause, assess, plan, act
PD	pharmacodynamics
PDA	personal digital assistant
PharmEc	pharmacoeconomics
PK	pharmacokinetics
PLG	pharma licensing group
R&D	research and development
RSS®	really simple syndication
SEC	Securities and Exchange Commission

SMART	Specific, Measurable, Achievable, Realistic and Timed objectives
SPC	specification of product characteristics
Specialty	pharmaceutical companies with a restricted therapeutic business area
SPV	special purpose vehicle
SUI	stress urinary incontinence
SWOT	Strengths, Weaknesses, Opportunities and Threats
TRIPS	trade-related aspects of intellectual property rights
VC	venture capital
WSJ	*Wall Street Journal*
WTO	World Trade Organization

Index

About the Author

Martin Austin founded TransformRx GmbH in January 2005 in response to observing the imbalance of information between companies and the investor community. Since then the company has been involved in advising funds and companies large and small on investment, merger, acquisition and business development issues. More information on the type and scope of these assignments can be found on the TransformRx website www.transformrx. com.

Management Education also forms a part of the TransformRx offer in conjunction with both C.E.L.forpharma in Brussels and ECPM at the University of Basel further information on these activities can also be found on the website.

In addition these activities have led to the formation of MarraM Advisors sàrl which has a special focus on the issue of governance in private equity financing and is engaged in the formation and structuring of a number of funds and now companies.

Martin Austin
Managing Director
TransformRx GmbH
mcaustin@transformrx.com